"People like that—nature as a force that humbles man and puts him in a proper perspective."
—Peter Stone, author of the '97 Broadway musical

Little WONDERS

In this volume you've met each of these remarkable people in the flower of their fame. Can you identify them when they were just sprouts? You'll find their names on Page 159. Using the numbers, match the acorns to the oaks

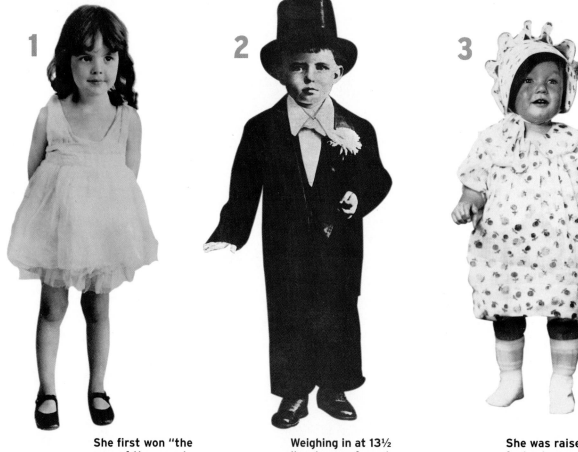

1 She first won "the roar of the crowd–that wonderful, wonderful sound" when she was 2.

2 Weighing in at 13½ lbs., he was feared stillborn until, held under a faucet, he wailed his first note.

3 She was raised in foster homes. The identity of her father has never been determined.

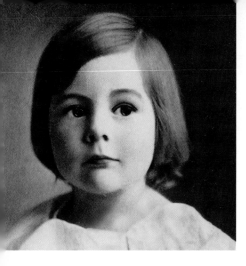

5 She grew up with handmade toys, horses and an English nanny.

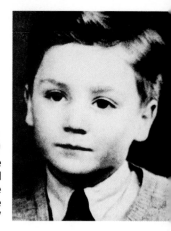

6 "He was always the one to dare you," said a boyhood friend. "He never cared what he said or did."

4 He and his sister, 18 months older, were dressed and treated as girl twins by their mother.

7 A baby-food ad with a sketch of his face by his artist mom was a household hit.

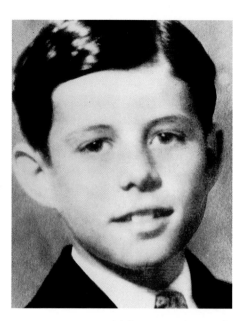

9 His prep-school classmates in 1935 voted him "most likely to succeed."

11 Her mother died when she was 3. She would perform for her adoring dad in improvised skits.

8 He failed twice to get into art school; it was downhill for society from there.

10 "She is the most beautiful creature I have ever seen in my life," exclaimed J.D. Salinger, after meeting her when she was 15.

12
After his mother's death from breast cancer when he was 9, he worked on his aunt and uncle's Indiana farm, and chased cows on a motorbike.

13
The lad and his older brother "would hear some pretty fiery arguments through the walls" after their father's benders.

14
Eloping at 16 got her expelled from boarding school.

15
"When one twin dies," his mother told him, "the one who lives gets the strength of both."

16
She had to learn to walk again after a bout of rheumatic fever at 17.

17
His abysmal grades and love of toy soldiers convinced his father he should pursue a military career.

18
Mother raised her by this rule: "Be just, be punctual, buy only what you need and pay cash."

19 He posed with his go-cart and an older pal. His gridiron skill would win him a USC scholarship.

20 An only child, he was doted upon by his mother, who moved to Boston to be near him when he went to Harvard.

21 The instrument whose name he took belonged to his grandmother. Retrieving it from her attic, he taught himself to play.

22 "Even when I was a tiny girl, I preferred being alone . . . I could give my imagination free rein and live in a world of lovely dreams."

23 Asthmatic and cerebral as a child, he would become famous for his outdoorsmanship.

24 "I never worry about the future," he (with his sister) said in his 60s. "It comes soon enough."

Match Numbers to the Names

___ Lucille Ball
___ Ingrid Bergman
___ Humphrey Bogart
___ Jacqueline Bouvier
___ Winston Churchill
___ James Dean
___ Albert Einstein
___ Greta Garbo
___ Judy Garland
___ Jean Harlow
___ Ernest Hemingway
___ Adolf Hitler
___ Grace Kelly
___ John F. Kennedy
___ John Lennon
___ Harpo Marx
___ Marilyn Monroe
___ Elvis Presley
___ Ronald Reagan
___ Franklin D. Roosevelt
___ Theodore Roosevelt
___ Frank Sinatra
___ Elizabeth Taylor
___ John Wayne

EVERETT COLLECTION (#S 12,13,14,15,17,18); ARCHIVE PHOTOS/POPPERFOTO (# 16)

INDEX

THE MOST INTRIGUING PEOPLE OF THE CENTURY

STAFF FOR THIS BOOK

EDITOR: Eric Levin

SENIOR EDITOR: Richard Burgheim

ART DIRECTOR: Miriam Campíz

SENIOR WRITERS: Tom Dunkel, Jill Smolowe

PICTURE EDITOR: Lynn Levine

CHIEF OF REPORTERS: Denise Lynch

CONTRIBUTING WRITERS: Alec Foege, Jamie Katz, J.D. Reed, Susan Schindehette, Sophronia Scott Gregory

REPORTERS: Averie LaRussa, Nanna Lydiker Stern

ART ASSISTANT: Gregg D. Baker

PHOTO ASSISTANT: Michael S. McHale

COPY EDITOR: Ricki Tarlow

OPERATIONS: Denise Doran

ADDITIONAL RESEARCH: Robert Britton, Steven Cook

Special thanks to Alan Anuskiewicz, John Calvano, Donna Cheng, Garry Clifford, Brien Foy, David Geithner, Erikka Haa, Villette Harris, George Hill, Suzy Im, Patricia R. Kornberg, Eric Mischel, Joseph Napolitano, James Oberman, Stephen Pabarue, Josef Siegle, Robert Vizzini, Angela Waters, Celine Wojtala, Liz Zale, the staff of Applied Graphics Technology and the PEOPLE Edit Tech staff.

MANAGING DIRECTOR: David Gitow

DIRECTOR, CONTINUITIES AND SINGLE SALES: David Arfine

DIRECTOR, CONTINUITIES: Michael Barrett

ASSISTANT DIRECTOR, CONTINUITIES: John Sandklev

PRODUCT MANAGERS: Robert Fox, Michael Holahan, Amy Jacobsson, Jennifer McLyman

MANAGER, RETAIL AND NEW MARKETS: Tom Mifsud

ASSOCIATE PRODUCT MANAGERS: Alison Ehrmann, Dan Melore, Pamela Paul, Charlotte Siddiqui, Allison Weiss, Dawn Weland

ASSISTANT PRODUCT MANAGERS: Alyse Daberko, Meredith Shelley, Betty Su

EDITORIAL OPERATIONS MANAGER: John Calvano

FULFILLMENT DIRECTOR: Michelle Gudema

FINANCIAL MANAGER: Tricia Griffin

ASSISTANT FINANCIAL MANAGER: Heather Lynds

MARKETING ASSISTANT: Lyndsay Jenks

CONSUMER MARKETING DIVISION

PRODUCTION DIRECTOR: John E. Tighe

BOOK PRODUCTION MANAGER: Donna Miano-Ferrara

ASSISTANT BOOK PRODUCTION MANAGER: Jessica McGrath

EDITOR-IN-CHIEF Norman Pearlstine
EDITORIAL DIRECTOR Henry Muller
EDITOR OF NEW MEDIA Daniel Okrent
TIME INC.
CHAIRMAN Reginald K. Brack Jr.
PRESIDENT, CEO Don Logan

MANAGING EDITOR Carol Wallace
EXECUTIVE EDITORS Cutler Durkee, Susan Toepfer
ASSISTANT MANAGING EDITORS Ross Drake, Charles Leerhsen, Roger R. Wolmuth, Jacob Young (Development)
EDITOR, SPECIAL PROJECTS Eric Levin
CHIEF OF CORRESPONDENTS Joe Treen
SENIOR EDITORS Max Alexander, Jack Friedman, Susan Hornik, Robert F. Howe, Bonnie Johnson, Jack Kelley (Los Angeles), Kristin McMurran, Mari McQueen, Janice Min, Ralph Novak, Joseph Poindexter, Elizabeth Sporkin
ART DIRECTOR John Shecut Jr.
PICTURE EDITOR Mary Carroll Marden
CHIEF OF REPORTERS Nancy Pierce Williamson
CHIEF OF STAFF Sarah Brody Janover
ASSOCIATE EDITORS Kim Cunningham, Thomas Fields-Meyer, Michelle Green, Kim Hubbard, George Kalogerakis, Michael A. Lipton, William Plummer, J.D. Reed, Leah Rozen, Karen S. Schneider
SENIOR WRITERS Peter Ames Carlin, Peter Castro, Steven Dougherty, Bruce Frankel, Tom Gliatto, Bill Hewitt, Richard Jerome, Pam Lambert, Steven Lang, Michael J. Neill, Curtis Rist, Patrick Rogers, Cynthia Sanz, Susan Schindehette
STAFF WRITERS Chuck Arnold, Sophronia Scott Gregory, Dan Jewel, Samantha Miller, Anne-Marie O'Neill, Lisa Russell, Kyle Smith, Alex Tresniowski, Joyce Wansley
WRITER-REPORTERS Andrew Abrahams (Deputy Chief), Veronica Burns, Denise Lynch (Deputies, Special Projects), Lisa Kay Greissinger, Mary S. Huzinec, Toby Kahn, Allison Lynn, Sabrina McFarland, Irene Kubota Neves, Maria Speidel
REPORTERS Greg Adkins, Marilyn Anderson, Amy Brooks, Jennifer Chrebet, David Cobb Craig, Rebecca Dameron, Amalia Duarte, Mary Green, Ann Guerin, Jeremy Helligar, Hugh McCarten, Erik Meers, Lan N. Nguyen, Gail Nussbaum, Vincent R. Peterson, Marisa Sandora, Mary Shaughnessy, Ying Sita, Brooke Bizzell Stachyra, Leslie Strauss, Jane Sugden, Randy Vest, Robin Ward
RESEARCH OPERATIONS James Oberman (Manager), Robert Britton, Steven Cook, Suzy Im, Céline Wojtala
PICTURE DEPARTMENT Beth Filler (Deputy), Maddy Miller (Deputy, Special Projects), Mary Fanette, Holly Holden, Ann Tortorelli (Associate Editors), Suzanne Cheruk, Mary Ellen Lidon, Lisa Morris, Josef Siegle, Eileen Sweet, John Toolan, Freyda Tavin, Mindy Viola, Blanche Williamson (Assistant Editors), Stan J. Williams (Picture Desk), Michael Brandson, Sara Guryan, Tom Mattie; Karin Grant, Michele Stueven (Los Angeles), Jerene Jones (London)
ART DEPARTMENT Hilli Pitzer (Deputy Director), Phil Simone (Special Projects Director), Helene Elek, Janice Hogan (Associate Directors), Angela Alleyne, Gregory Monfries (Assistant Directors), Tom Allison, Ronnie Brandwein, Michelle Angelee Smith (Designers), Allan D. Bintliff Sr., Nora Cassar, Charles Castillo, Brien Foy, Joseph Randazzo
COPY DESK Patricia R. Kornberg (Chief), Will Becker (Deputy), Judith I. Fogarty, Rose Kaplan (Copy Coordinators), Hollis C. Bernard, William Doares, Ben Harte, Alan Levine, Mary C. Radich, Muriel C. Rosenblum, Sheryl F. Stein (Copy Editors), Lillian Nici, Deborah Ratel, Patricia Rommeney, Joanann Scali (Assistants)
OPERATIONS Alan Anuskiewicz (Manager), Liz Zale (Deputy), Michael G. Aponte, Donna Cheng, Denise M. Doran, Erikka V. Haa, George W. Hill, Michelle Lockhart, Key Martin, Ali Namvar, Mia Rublowska, Ellen Shapiro, Larry Whiteford
TECHNOLOGY Eric Mischel (Director), Esther Chang, Scott Damm, Thomas Fitzgibbon, Janine Gordon, Fred Kao, Cheroc Lawless, Gregory Paik, Alison Sawyer, Anthony White
PRODUCTION Robert Bronzo, Paul Castrataro, Thomas C. Colaprico, Geri Flanagan, Paul Zelinski (Managers), Catherine Barron, David Pandy, Kathleen Seery, Anthony White
IMAGING Betsy Castillo (Manager), Willis Caster Jr. (Assistant Manager), Warren Thompson (Supervisor), Steven Cadicamo, Paul Dovell, Robert Fagan, Francis Fitzgerald, Patricia Fitzgerald Gordon, Kevin Grimstead, Henry Groskinsky, James M. Lello, Brian Luckey, Anthony G. Moore, Craig Puffer, Joanne Recca, Robert Roszkowski, Randall Swift, Peter Tylus, Victor Van Carpels, Susan Vroom
DIRECTOR, NEW MEDIA Hala Makowska
NEW MEDIA DEPARTMENT Dylan Jones (Editor, PEOPLE Online), Heather Craig, Lorraine Goods, Heather White (Picture Editor)
PUBLIC AFFAIRS Susan Ollinick (Director), Dianne Jones, Sheri Wohl Lapidus
EDITORIAL BUSINESS MANAGER David Geithner, Orpha Davis (Deputy)
ADMINISTRATION Susan E. Baldwin, Bernard Acquaye, Isabel Alves, Xiomara D. Cotton, Nancy Eils, Rayna L. Evans, Joy Fordyce, Deirdre Gallagher, Ruth Oden, Marie L. Parker, Mari Parks, Jean Reynolds, Shirley Van Putten, Martha White, Maureen S. Fulton (Letters/Syndication Manager)
NEWS BUREAU Sarah Skolnik (Deputy Chief), J.D. Podolsky (News Editor), Anna Lisa Raya, William Brzozowski, Richard G. Williams
NATIONAL CORRESPONDENT: Giovanna Breu
DOMESTIC BUREAUS CHICAGO, Cindy Dampier (Chief), Luchina Fisher, Joanne Fowler Lorna Grisby, Leisa Marthaler; **HOUSTON,** Anne Maier (Chief), Donna Buchala; **LOS ANGELES,** Todd Gold (Deputy Chief), Shelley Levitt, Craig Tomashoff (Associate Chiefs), Lorenzo Benet, Karen Brailsford, Thomas Cunneff, Johnny Dodd, John Hannah, Danelle Morton, Vicki Sheff-Cahan, Lyndon Stambler, Lynda Wright, Paula Yoo, Florence Nishida, Alison Brown, Monica Clark, Cecilia de la Paz; **MIAMI,** Meg Grant (Chief), Marisa Salcines, Leslie Marine; **NEW YORK,** Kristen Kelch (Chief), Ron Arias, Anthony Duignan-Cabrera, Maria Eftimiades, Nancy Matsumoto, Elizabeth F. McNeil, Cynthia Wang, Mercedes Mitchell; **WASHINGTON,** Garry Clifford (Chief), Linda Kramer, Margie Bonnett Sellinger, Vornida Seng, Angela Waters
EUROPEAN EDITOR Fred Hauptfuhrer
EUROPEAN BUREAU Lydia Denworth (Chief), Bryan Alexander, Nina A. Biddle, Simon Perry
SPECIAL CORRESPONDENTS ALBUQUERQUE, Michael Haederle; **ATLANTA,** Gail Wescott; **BOSTON,** Tom Duffy, Stephen Sawicki; **CHICAGO,** Barbara Sandler; **DENVER,** Vickie Bane; **DETROIT,** Fannie Weinstein; **JERUSALEM,** Abe Rabinovich; **LONDON,** Joanna Blonska, Margaret Wright; **LOS ANGELES,** Mitchell Fink, Anne-Marie Otey, Jeff Schaufer; **MEMPHIS/NASHVILLE,** Jane Sanderson; **MIAMI,** Don Sider; **MINNEAPOLIS,** Margaret Nelson; **NEW YORK,** Anne Longley; **PARIS,** Cathy Nolan; **ROME,** Toula Vlahou; **SAN ANTONIO,** Joseph Harmes, Bob Stewart; **SALT LAKE CITY,** Cathy Free; **WASHINGTON,** Mary Esselman, Jennifer Mendelsohn, Jane Sims Podesta
CONTRIBUTING PHOTOGRAPHERS Harry Benson, Ian Cook, Stephen Ellison, Acey Harper, Steve Kagan, Christopher Little, Jim McHugh, Robin Platzer, Neal Preston, Co Rentmeester, Mark Sennet, Peter Serling, Barry Staver, Dale Wittner, Taro Yamasaki
TIME INC.
EXECUTIVE EDITORS: Joëlle Attinger, José M. Ferrer III
DEVELOPMENT EDITOR: Isolde Motley
EDITORIAL SERVICES Sheldon Czapnik (Director), Claude Boral (General Manager); Thomas E. Hubbard (Photo Lab); Lany Walden McDonald (Research Center); Beth Bencini Zarcone (Picture Collection); Thomas Smith (Technology); James Macove (Marketing); Maryann Kornely (Syndication)
EDITORIAL TECHNOLOGY Paul Zazzera (Vice President); Damien Creavin (Director)

PRESIDENT Ann S. Moore
VICE PRESIDENT Jeremy B. Koch
CONSUMER MARKETING DIRECTOR Greg Harris
BUSINESS MANAGER Robert D. Jurgrau
PRODUCTION DIRECTOR Tracy T. Windrum

PUBLISHER Nora P. McAniff
ASSOCIATE PUBLISHER/ADVERTISING Peter Bauer
ASSOCIATE PUBLISHER/MARKETING Vanessa Reed
ADVERTISING DIRECTOR John J. Gallagher

Preceding page, from top left: Bob Dylan, 1964; Katharine Hepburn, ca. 1936; Charles Lindbergh, 1927; Gilda Radner, 1980

112

CONTENTS

36

Marilyn reflects,
1953; Louis
projects, 1966.

The *The* Public EYE

The lens and the mike made all the world a glittering stage, catapulting a new creature, the Celebrity, to instant impact

I N THE BEGINNING, THERE WAS THE WORD, BUT NO PIC-tures. And though all the beasts of the field were created in just a week, the world had to wait 20 centuries for the genesis of the Celebrity. The Lord had not said, Let there be limelight. Indeed until the early 1800s, heroes and the buzz about them clip-clopped from town to town on the back of a horse. Then mass communications transformed the velocity, criteria and impact of fame. In the process, the glare of recognition became an ambiguous blessing. At the top of the staircase of stardom might lurk an ambush of paparazzi (as Elizabeth Taylor found, left, in 1968). As the media grew and the line blurred between public and private, highbrow and low-brow, what came to be known as pop culture emerged.

This book celebrates the beacons of that culture. The names are not always the Most Significant. Rather, these are the figures who most memorably captured our attention—sometimes tragi-cally, alas, by their villainy. Together, their tales constitute a com-pelling narrative of this, the first century of celebrity.

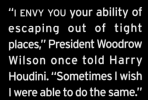

"I ENVY YOU your ability of escaping out of tight places," President Woodrow Wilson once told Harry Houdini. "Sometimes I wish I were able to do the same."

In devising such mind-boggling spectacles as the Chinese Water Torture Cell, the Nude Jail Cell Escape and the Underwater Handcuff Escape (left, in Boston, 1906), Houdini raised carny skills to a gripping metaphor for the human struggle. Perhaps his greatest feat was his invention of himself. Born in Budapest in 1874, Erik Weisz was one of five children of a penniless emigrant rabbi who died when Erik was 18. As Harry Houdini, he would become undisputed master of the strenuous, death-defying art he termed "self-liberation." He railed against psychic shackles too—anti-Semitism and the séance craze of the early 1900s.

But though he enjoyed a long and loving marriage, Houdini never broke free of one thing: his fanatical devotion to his mother, Cecilia. "I am what would be called a mother's-boy," he once conceded. "If I do anything, I say to myself I wonder if Ma would want me to do this." When he died of peritonitis at 52, on Halloween, 1926, his casket was adorned with a wreath that spelled MOTHER LOVE, and his head lay on a pillow of Cecilia's letters.

KING CONNECTED WITH HIS FLOCK TO MAKE HIS DREAM REAL

AS A CHILD in Georgia, Martin Luther King Jr. rode trains in which curtains were drawn to keep black and white passengers from dining together. "I felt just as if a curtain had come down across my whole life," he once said. "The insult of it I will never forget." As an adult, King endeavored to tear down the curtain between those two separate and unequal Americas. In 1963 he was in Baltimore, reaching out from his motorcade to greet his grassroots supporters. A year later he was in Stockholm, collecting the Nobel Peace Prize in the presence of Norwegian and Swedish royalty. Whether from the steps of the Lincoln Memorial or the dank confines of an Alabama jail, King put his ideals ahead of his physical safety—and ultimately paid with his life. "Right temporarily defeated," he proclaimed in his Nobel acceptance speech, "is stronger than evil triumphant."

CALLED BY DYLAN, YOUTH BATTLED AGE-OLD INJUSTICE

IN TIMES ABLAZE with change and social reform, the firebrands were folksingers. Woody Guthrie was the wandering minstrel of the Great Depression, his "This Land Is Your Land" helping to lift the dark despair of the Dust Bowl. Three decades later, a 22-year-old Bob Dylan plucked a tune for civil rights workers in the Jim Crow domain of Mississippi during the tinderbox summer of '63. His "Blowin' in the Wind" stirred a generation and built a bridge between blacks and whites, becoming an unofficial anthem of the fight for racial redress.

DANNY LYON/MAGNUM

SATCHMO CONQUERED NEW ORLEANS, THEN THE WORLD

THE SOUND OF his horn was penetrating and ecstatic. So was the power of his smile. Born in poverty to a granddaughter of slaves, Louis Armstrong had an irrepressibly independent spirit that both landed him in a New Orleans juvenile home and catapulted him to center stage at London's Palladium, where he called to King George V, "This one's for you, Rex." The world's goodwill ambassador of jazz, Armstrong understood his mission well, as was evident when he serenaded orphans in Cairo in 1961. "I'm there," he once said, "in the cause of happiness. And I don't worry what nobody thinks."

ELVIS EMOTED WHILE HIS MENTOR MADE THE IDOL RICH

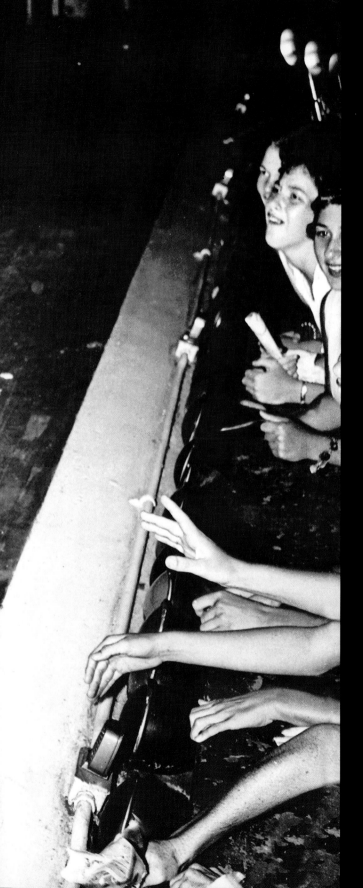

FOR ELVIS PRESLEY, per-forming was a fairly inde-scribable experience. "It's like your whole body gets goose bumps, but it's not goose bumps," he once said. "It's not a chill either. It's like a surge of electricity going through you. It's al-most like making love, but it's even stronger than that."

On the other side of the footlights the experience was nearly as powerful. And Col. Tom Parker, Elvis's crafty manager, wanted to keep it that way. Which is why, the morning after Elvis howled "Don't Be Cruel" at Miami's Olympia Theatre, in August 1956 (left), Parker was steamed to see Elvis's steady at the time—an 18-year-old beauty from Biloxi named June Juanico—quoted in the paper describing the depth of her love for him. "Son, we can't have this kind of publicity," Parker said. Presley certainly cared for June, but he cared for his image more, and he rarely disobeyed the Colonel. Later that day, Presley assured a reporter: "I got 25 girls I date regular." Hello, Heartbreak Hotel.

DON WRIGHT

HOISTED TO HEROISM, CHURCHILL DEFINED LEADERSHIP

THE GOOD TIMES were rolling in Britain when Winston Churchill—combat vet, author, painter, bon vivant and Tory MP—was named chancellor of Bristol University in 1930. Frisky students celebrated by parading their beloved Winnie about town. The giddy mood was short-lived, though, perishing in the savage blitzkrieg of the Nazi war machine. Within a decade, those once jolly boys of Bristol marched off to defend Europe, and Churchill was called to 10 Downing Street to take the lead in what he so eloquently exhorted them to make the Empire's "finest hour."

EINSTEIN COGITATED COSMICALLY, BUT HE LIVED DOWN-TO-EARTH

"IT STRIKES ME as unfair, and even in bad taste, to select a few individuals for boundless admiration, attributing superhuman powers of mind and character to them," Albert Einstein said in a 1921 interview. "This has been my fate, and the contrast between the popular estimate of [me] and the reality is simply grotesque." If the scientist who rewrote our understanding of time, matter and energy was being characteristically modest, it was because he was as much in awe of the "magnificent structure" of the universe as ordinary people were of him. He once called himself "a deeply religious nonbeliever." Tempered by two world wars and the Jewish persecution that brought him to the U.S. from Germany in the '30s, Einstein (who died in 1955 at age 76) became an ardent pacifist and proponent of world government. He knew he was not a leader himself, however, and in 1952 declined the presidency of Israel. Einstein cared little for money (he once used a $1,500 check as a bookmark and then lost the book) or fashion (he moved about Princeton without socks or tie, a blue stocking cap on his head). Next to numbers, he felt most at ease with kids. When a young cousin (second from left) visited his home with some refugees in 1949, the old physicist lit up like a department-store Santa.

AP

IN THE FACE OF GANDHI'S PASSIVE RESISTANCE, THE EMPIRE STRUCK THE FLAG

MOHANDAS GANDHI—an ascetic, loincloth-clad, London-trained lawyer—led the civil-disobedience campaign that ended the nearly two-century British raj in India. Enduring hunger strikes and a dozen years in jail, he deployed what he called "soul force," or conquering through love and nonviolence—concepts he credited to sources ranging from the New Testament to Thoreau.

Tragically, India erupted in bloody sectarian strife after evicting the colonialists in 1947. "The time was when whatever I said the masses followed," he sighed on his 78th birthday in 1947. "Today I am a lone voice in India."

Nonetheless, Gandhi continued to travel the land to preach tolerance to groups like the Muslims depicted here. But four months after his birthday, in January 1948, while en route to a prayer meeting, he was gunned down by an extremist of his own Hindu faith. Yet Gandhi's doctrine of strategic non-violent protest lived on in such far-flung disciples as Nelson Mandela and Martin Luther King Jr.

UPI/CORBIS-BETTMANN

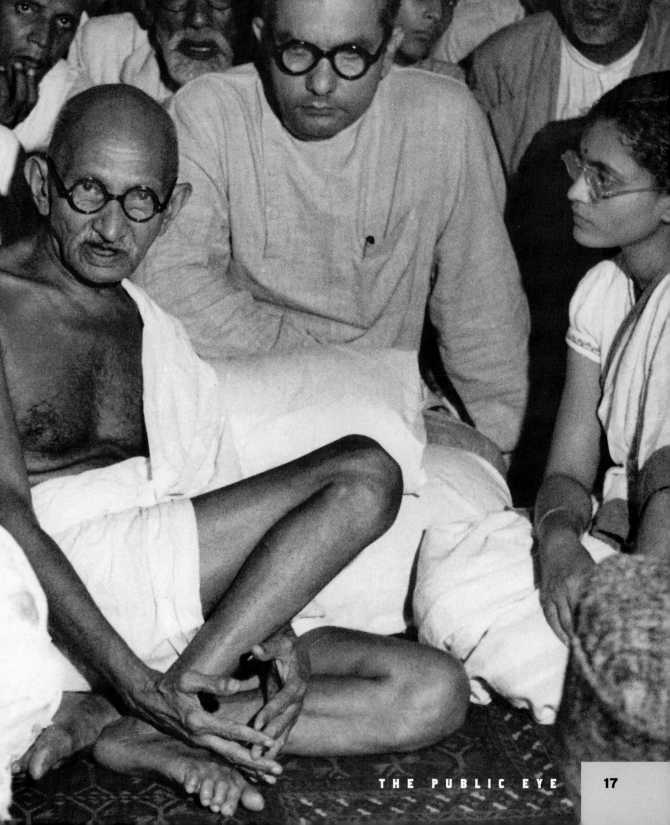

MONROE PUT THE TROOPS INTO BOMBSHELL SHOCK

IN THE TRADITION of Bob Hope and the USO troupes of World War II, actress-pinup queen Marilyn Monroe brought cheer and what was then called cheesecake to more than 100,000 GIs in South Korea in 1954. The delirious audiences—several soldiers were nearly trampled charging the stage—were the stuff of a performer's dreams. It was an exultant moment for Monroe, a time to revel in her fame before it came to destroy her eight years later. As she gushed upon returning home, "I never felt like a star before in my heart."

MADONNA PRESENTS A HALL OF MIRRORS FOR JADED TIMES

DISPLAYING THE LATEST in Media Dominatrix evening wear, Madonna arrived at the 1991 Cannes Film Festival for a screening of her docu-melodrama, *Truth or Dare*. But that, of course, was just the image du jour for this restless maestro of self-reinvention and self-promotion. Brazen with a wink, the singer-actress-producer emerged as one of the highest-paid female entertainers of all time. Don't bet that motherhood, which came in 1996 at 38, will mellow her. As she once said, "It's better to live one year as a tiger than 100 as a sheep." Grrrrr.

HANK AND DI AND COLIN AND BABS TAKE MANHATTAN

CELEBRITY PROVED DEMOCRATIC for a German boy who fled the Nazis; a demure British kindergarten aide; a son of Jamaican immigrants; and a painfully shy Florida girl. They found themselves together in their black-and-white best at a 1995 New York City benefit for United Cerebral Palsy. As Princess Diana and Gen. Colin Powell received awards from Henry Kissinger and Barbara Walters, no one was more starstruck than the celebs themselves.

"This generation of Americans has a rendezvous with destiny."
—FDR

The First Couple seemed exultant in 1941 after the third of FDR's four inaugurals.

They dazzled and delighted, influenced and inspired. When bewitched by the blinding glow radiated by each of these luminaries, the world seemed both a more enchanting and a less daunting place to live

Larger *Than* Life

ELEANOR & FRANKLIN ROOSEVELT

The 32d President offered Americans a New Deal—and his wife a raw one

ON THE DAY IN 1905 THAT NEW YORK SOCIALITE ELEANOR ROOSEVELT HEADED down the aisle on the arm of her uncle, then-President Theodore Roosevelt, neither she nor the recent Harvard graduate who awaited her at the altar, her fifth cousin Franklin, could have foreseen the trials and triumphs that awaited them. By the time FDR took over the Oval Office 28 years later with the fighting words, "First of all, let me assert my firm belief that the only thing we have to fear is fear itself," both partners already knew personally the crushing weight of fear.

Born to privilege and the sporting life, FDR was stricken at 39 with polio, encumbering him thereafter with braces and a wheelchair. He emerged from six years of rehab with the determined optimism that would later help him lead the nation out of its

malaise and against the ravages of the Depression and the Axis powers. He left behind Social Security and a safety net for the poor.

Eleanor, meanwhile, stepped in as FDR's eyes, ears and legs, particularly during World War II when she toured battlefields and hospital wards to support the troops. She not only penned a newspaper column and raised six children but served as champion of the downtrodden and of human rights. Behind her dynamism, though, was the pain of a woman trapped in a marriage to a philandering husband who held on largely for the sake of his political career. In 1918, Eleanor learned that FDR was having an affair with her social secretary Lucy Mercer. With that discovery, she would write years later, "the bottom dropped out of my own particular world." Just as FDR (in a conspiracy with the press unthinkable today) hid his disability from the public, Eleanor masked her marital estrangement—and, it is rumored, a lesbian liaison. Thus, the Roosevelts proved to be not only the century's greatest President and First Lady but also the century's ultimate Power Couple. ■

Even on the hustings, FDR tried to hide his handicap. Eleanor (here visiting a progressive school) served as plenipotentiary to the forgotten. At 77, she headed a commission on the status of women.

THEODORE ROOSEVELT

*All guts and gusto,
he boosted ecology and
wielded the 'big stick'*

WHETHER HE WAS storming an enemy hill in Cuba, bagging rhinoceri in Africa, riding on his ranch, or writing one of his 38 books, America's 26th President exhibited a swashbuckling zeal that he once aptly described as "going hard at everything." A fervent nationalist, moralist and conservationist, as well as an adept populist, the man fondly known to voters as Teddy was hell-bent on ensuring a "square deal" for all American citizens. His insatiable hunger for the limelight provoked detractors to joke that when T.R. went to a funeral, he resented the corpse.

Born asthmatic and puny, Roosevelt early on developed a view of the world as a place to be conquered. At 25, he lost both his mother and his wife on Valentine's Day to fatal illnesses. After a three-year hiatus from public life to play the role of lonesome cowboy, he roared back to politics and took a new wife, with whom he raised six kids. ∎

CORBIS-BETTMANN

"I am as strong as a bull moose, and you can use me up to the limit." —His campaign credo

APRIL 16, 1889 – DECEMBER 25, 1977
CHARLIE CHAPLIN

Walking an inimitable walk, he was king of the silents

Good-time Charlie finally settled down with wife Oona, mother of eight of his 10 kids, including (below in 1948) Michael and actress-to-be Geraldine. In 1940 he belatedly made his first talkie, cavorting as Adenoid Hynkel in *The Great Dictator*.

CHARLIE CHAPLIN STRUCK IT RICH BY PLAYING POOR. His recurring "Little Tramp" character—he of the bowler hat, caterpillar mustache and never-ending run of bad luck—tip-toed the lines between comedy and tragedy. George Bernard Shaw declared him "the one genius created by the cinema." Young Charlie spent two years in an orphanage and danced for pennies in the streets of London before emigrating to Hollywood in 1913. Through the '20s and '30s, Chaplin wrote, directed and starred in silent-era masterpieces like *The Gold Rush* and *Modern Times* that first pushed evolving film comedy beyond slapstick.

Offscreen his life was a tabloid editor's delight: The Svengali-esque auteur stirred controversy with four marriages to teenage brides as well as with his pro-Soviet politics. "I am not a Communist," he informed the House Un-American Activities Committee. "I am what you call a peacemonger." And in 1952 a bitter Chaplin moved to Switzerland with his fourth wife, Oona, the daughter of playwright Eugene O'Neill. Reconciliation came 20 years later when he returned to Hollywood to accept an honorary Academy Award for "making motion pictures the art form of this century." Unlike his hapless Tramp, Chaplin's life had a happy ending. ■

TOP: THE KOBAL COLLECTION; BOTTOM LEFT: JOHN ENGSTEAD/MPTPA .; BOTTOM RIGHT: REX FEATURES LTD.

"The little chap," he said of his alter ego, "wears the air of romantic hunger."

"I've just done what I damn well wanted to . . . and I ain't afraid of being alone."

Her mysterious smile in this 1941 still provided ample response to Dorothy Parker's famous putdown that Hepburn's acting "ran the gamut of emotions from A to B."

NOVEMBER 9, 1907 –

KATHARINE
HEPBURN

*Undeterred by directors, designers or moralizers,
she handled Hollywood and the world her way*

KATE HEPBURN NEVER WAS ONE TO SUFFER FOOLS LIGHT-
ly. When a gossip columnist phoned her home in 1995 to
confirm a report that the screen legend was in failing
health, Hepburn snapped, "Trying to see if I'm dead yet?" and
hung up. That crusty, waspish wit and sword-crossing honesty is
precisely what endears Hepburn to audiences. During a Hollywood career that spanned five decades, produced 44 films and
garnered an unparalleled four Oscars, Hepburn never did it any
way but her own. A patrician of Yankee stock, Hepburn had a
highfalutin sound and angular look that failed to catch fire during
her first tour of Hollywood in the '30s. Branded "box-office poison,"
she returned East with her then-boyfriend, millionaire Howard
Hughes. Following a star turn in the Broadway premiere of *The
Philadelphia Story*, Hepburn returned to Hollywood, this time
hell-bent on custom-tailoring her screen and real-life roles without regard to reigning conventions. The only rival authority in
her life was the man with whom she made the battle of the sexes
magical for moviegoers: Spencer Tracy. Yet she battled neither his
alcoholism nor his failure to divorce his estranged wife. "I would
have done anything for him," she stated simply. ∎

Off the set, as
well as on the
1936 shoot of
Sylvia Scarlett
(lower left),
Hepburn
favored the
androgynous
allure and com-
fort of man-
tailored clothes.
In 1967, she
filmed *Guess
Who's Coming
to Dinner?*
(below), the last
of her nine
movies with
real-life love
Spencer Tracy.

"Everyone is the age he has decided on, and I have decided to remain 30," quoth the master at 76.

A man of many muses, he worked with Lydia Corbett and (below) socialized with first wife Olga Koklova in 1919.

OCTOBER 25,1881–APRIL 8,1973

PABLO PICASSO

With Dionysian force and monumental strokes, he illumined our age

LEFT: DAVID DOUGLAS DUNCAN; TOP RIGHT: ARCHIVE PHOTOS/POPPERFOTO ; BOTTOM RIGHT: GLOBE PHOTOS

S O PROTEAN WAS HIS ART, SO VAST HIS INFLUENCE, SO TITANIC HIS PERSON- ality, that at the time of his death in 1973, Pablo Picasso was extolled as the preeminent artist of the 20th century. "He is the last artist in this century who will dominate the scene, who will have been a real king during his lifetime," eulogized American painter Robert Motherwell. Picasso's true legacy, of course, is the avalanche of work he left behind, a collection of more than 6,000 paintings and 1,200 sculptures that unsettled with their mind-bending juxtapositions of human and mythic forms, unique linear distortions and original way of positing the–or, more accurately, *his*–universe. "I don't want there to be three or four thousand possibilities of interpreting my canvas," he said. "I want there to be only one." The same prodigious appetites that fueled his creative output produced a succession of mistresses, seven of whom proved significant to his work and life, two of whom he married, three of whom bore him children. All of them he dubbed "goddesses or doormats." ∎

He twirled in a sort of satyr's gavotte in 1957, in a French Riviera base established after leaving his native Spain.

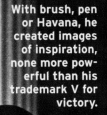

With brush, pen or Havana, he created images of inspiration, none more powerful than his trademark V for victory.

CECIL BEATON

WINSTON CHURCHILL

His words like lightning in a dark time, this man truly was an island

THE GREATEST STATESMAN OF THE CENTURY GREW UP IN A 320-ROOM CAS-tle, a scion of an ancestor of the first Duke of Marlborough and an American heiress. Though Winston Churchill stuttered as a child and barely got into military college, he distinguished himself as a soldier, and entered Parliament at 26. Forced from the Cabinet during World War I for urging the ultimately calamitous Gallipoli campaign, he presciently spurred development of the tank and warned that the punitive Versailles Treaty would only embitter Germany. When the Nazis proved him right and war came in 1939, his authority and oratory as Prime Minister turned the tide. With his wife Clementine at his side for 57 years, Churchill lived on to rail against the Soviet threat (coining the term Iron Curtain) and earn a Nobel Prize for his volumes of biography and history. FDR once cabled his brandy-chugging comrade in arms: "It's fun to be in the same decade with you." ∎

"We shall fight in the seas and oceans . . . we shall fight in the fields and in the streets . . . we shall never surrender."

"I have always felt I was using the five senses within me."

HELEN KELLER

Her accomplishments continue to astonish, enthrall and inspire

FOR HELEN KELLER, IT WAS NEVER ENOUGH SIMPLY TO "HEAR" THROUGH HER fingertips or to "see" with her acute sense of smell. When she wanted a closer "look," Keller would proceed fearlessly, stroking a lion's mouth or inviting a snake to wrap itself around her. "I seldom think about my limitations," she once said, "and they never make me sad."

Nearly everyone knows about the magical moment, immortalized in William Gibson's *The Miracle Worker*, when an unruly 6-year-old Helen connected to the word "water" and was thus freed from her dark, silent loneliness. But that epiphany was only the beginning of a life that proved remarkable by any standard. Propelled by an unflagging optimism and insatiable curiosity, Keller had mastered French and German, Greek and Latin, Shakespeare and the Christian doctrines of Swedenborg, by the time she graduated cum laude from Radcliffe in the class of '04. Her multifaceted career included publishing 14 books, turns on the vaudeville stage and Socialist lecture circuit, as well as tireless campaigning on behalf of the deaf and blind. ∎

Opposite page: In the early '50s a pawnbroker returned a braille watch she had lost in a New York City taxicab.

LEFT: LARRY BURROWS/LIFE; MIDDLE: AP; RIGHT: NINA LEEN/LIFE

"If I could see, I would marry first of all," Keller said after her mother broke up her one love affair.

When she played Keller in *The Miracle Worker* in 1961, Patty Duke, 15, paid her an admiring visit.

LOUIS ARMSTRONG

The founding father of jazz spread a message of joy to the world

SHINING THROUGH THAT FAMOUS TWO-OCTAVE SMILE WAS THE WORLD'S first acknowledged African-American musical genius—a man whose startling trumpet solos and ebulliently growling vocals freed melody for spontaneous flight and set toes tapping. Few could resist the warmth of his music—or personality. On a visit to Pope Paul VI in 1968, Satchmo was asked if he had children. "No, Father," he reportedly replied. "But I sure had a lot of fun tryin'." A road warrior for five decades, Armstrong cut 2,000 records and starred on stage, screen, radio, TV and even in a Betty Boop cartoon. In later years, some objected to his old-fashioned mugging on stage, often unaware of his principled stands on civil rights. (He once canceled a State Department tour of the USSR over federal inaction on desegregation.) Pops chose to live modestly with Lucille, his fourth wife, in a lower-middle-class section of Queens, New York, "to be with my people." Duke Ellington gave him this salute: "I loved and respected Louis Armstrong. He was born poor, died rich, and never hurt anyone along the way." ∎

In 1956, above, the toll the trumpet took on his lips was evident. "It's been hard goddamn work, man," Satchmo declared in 1969.

Pops relaxed backstage in 1959. Once asked to explain his extraordinary global appeal, he replied, "A note's a note in any language!"

Said Dizzy Gillespie, speaking for all jazz and pop artists: "No him, no me."

37

AUGUST 25,1918–OCTOBER 14,1990

LEONARD BERNSTEIN

A mercurial maestro brought classical music to the masses

PIANIST, COMPOSER, CONDUCTOR, AND WILD MAN ABOUT TOWN, LEONARD Bernstein was an orchestra of divided selves. When he died of heart failure caused by decades of chain-smoking and chain-working, a friend noted, "Lenny led four lives in one, so he was not 72, but 288." Despite not touching a piano until he was 10, Bernstein became at 25 an assistant conductor with the New York Philharmonic. His stage style was so animated that on several occasions he toppled off his podium. Bernstein's private life was equally histrionic. Though married with three children, he was openly bisexual. Critics charged that the profligate, prodigiously gifted composer of *West Side Story* and *Candide* pursued too many muses, and Bernstein pled guilty: "I don't want to spend my life, as Toscanini did, studying and restudying the same 50 pieces of music. It would bore me to death." ■

"Without him, we'd have a lot of holes in our culture." —Quincy Jones

> "A man can be defeated but not destroyed."
> —*The Old Man and the Sea*

JULY 21,1899–JULY 2,1961

ERNEST HEMINGWAY

Macho prose and a two-fisted life made him a literary heavyweight

The physical and intellectual standards he tried to adhere to put a premium on what he called "grace under pressure."

CLARENCE HEMINGWAY GAVE HIS SON A FISHING ROD AT AGE 3 AND A SHOT-gun at 10. Clearly, the boy was not going to be a couch potato. Ernest Hemingway—soldier, sinner, war correspondent, big-game fisherman and hunter—lived large on three continents. And wrote about his experiences in a revolutionary taut style. "Prose is architecture," he declared, "not interior decoration." Hemingway fought (literally) with his editor, hit the bars and bullfights, machine-gunned sharks from his boat and took four wives. But the short stories and novels piled up too, earning him a Nobel Prize and worldwide acclaim. The end was ugly. Very Hemingway. Physical decline and depression didn't suit "Papa," and at 61 he did what his father had done: put a gun to his head and pulled the trigger. (His granddaughter Margaux would take her own life 35 years later.) "His destiny," noted one critic, "has been to symbolize an age of unparalleled violence as no other American has symbolized it." ∎

TOP: JAY LEVITON/ATLANTA; BOTTOM: L-R: SIPA PRESS; UPI/CORBIS-BETTMANN; BOB WILLOUGHBY/MPTPA; EVERETT COLLECTION

JANUARY 8,1935–AUGUST 16,1977

ELVIS PRESLEY

Rock and roll's King is dead, long live the King!

H E COULDN'T CLAIM THE ETHEREAL MOAN of a Roy Orbison, the greased-lightning guitar of a Chuck Berry or the polished presentation of a Pat Boone. All he did, it seemed, was shake people up. "Popular music has reached its lowest depths in the 'grunt and groin' antics of one Elvis Presley," harrumphed the New York *Daily News*. "He's not my cup of tea," sniffed the talking coat-hanger Ed Sullivan, even as he scrambled to book the bedroom-eyed teen idol who quivered and quaked like a carnal Krakatoa. Presley, the poor boy from Tupelo and Memphis, unleashed the seditious spirit of rock and roll, but he was not really a rebel. The Hillbilly Cat didn't drink or smoke. When the Army called, he went. By the 1970s, after his acting and singing careers endured seismic ups and downs, he became poignantly square—he played Vegas, begged President Nixon to issue him a narc's badge and let him fight "drug abuse and communist brainwashing," and even refused to wear jeans. In his drug-addled and depressed final days, burrowed in the ornate cradle of Graceland, his family life shattered, the King must have wondered whether he had a future. If only he had known then what we know now: 50 million Elvis impersonators can't be wrong. ∎

On the road, Elvis (in 1956) would call his mother, Gladys, daily because "she's not in real good health, anyway, and if she worries too much, it might not be good for her."

40

"On the one hand, he exuded untamed sexuality. On the other, he was like a pious little choirboy." —Linda Thompson, Elvis's last live-in love

From far left: Private Presley toted his duffle in Germany, 1958; Elvis and wife Priscilla welcomed Lisa Marie, 1968; Sophia Loren spied him in the Paramount commissary, 1958, and helped herself; on TV in 1973, the first rococo rocker bid *Aloha from Hawaii.*

MUHAMMAD ALI

The brash boxer-versifier who dubbed himself 'The Greatest' wasn't talkin' trash

HE NO LONGER STINGS LIKE A bee, and Muhammad Ali– three-time heavyweight champion of the world–says of life after Parkinson's syndrome, "Now [people] feel sorry for me. They thought I was Superman. Now they can go, 'He's human, like us.'" There was a time Ali seemed invincible. He was the first athlete to master the media and out-talk Howard Cosell. He resisted the Vietnam draft, ex- plaining, "I ain't got no quarrel with those Viet Cong," and as a Muslim conscientious objector, he eluded prison. "It's just another test," Ali says of his affliction, and he's passing with flying colors. Witness when he lit the '96 Olympic flame with his hum- mingbird arms. The entourage is gone (replaced by his fourth wife, with whom he adopted the last of his nine kids). The strength has faded. But Ali is still the world champ, on the road for charities 275 days a year. He just doesn't box anymore. ∎

> "Birds fly,
> waves
> pound the
> sand. I beat
> people up."

In flapper fur, Ruth went out en famille in 1931.

"I hit big or I miss big. I like to live as big as I can."

Still using his "slavemaster name," Cassius Clay clinched with his $1 million purse for the '64 Sonny Liston bout.

FEBRUARY 6, 1895 – AUGUST 16, 1948

BABE RUTH

The Bambino was point man for America's jock culture

GEORGE HERMAN "BABE" RUTH WAS THE PROTOTYPE OF THE SPORTS superstar. On and off the field. "I don't room with him," a teammate quipped. "I room with his suitcase." Despite his carousing, Ruth was one of the game's great pitchers before he became its preeminent slugger. Raised in a Baltimore Catholic school for delinquents, the Babe sobered somewhat after his first wife died and he wed a former Ziegfeld girl. And in World War II, long after his retirement, he was such an international legend that Japanese troops, as they crossed the battle lines, yelled at GIs, "To hell with Babe Ruth!" ∎

TOP LEFT: GEORGE ZENO COLLECTION; TOP RIGHT: LOOMIS DEAN/LIFE; BOTTOM: RAY JONES/MPTPA

Lucy and Desi (above, in 1953) made a stormy couple. On *I Love Lucy,* her wacky originality (above right, with Mary Wickes) made audiences forget her sultrier days on the silver screen (below in 1940).

AUGUST 6, 1911 – APRIL 26, 1989

LUCILLE BALL

Ditzy on-air, canny off, her legacy of laughter will rerun forever

NO TV PERFORMER BEFORE OR SINCE HAS BEEN SO DEARLY LOVED AS LUCY. Viewers adored her Raggedy Ann looks, her raucous guffaw. Mostly, though, they worshipped Lucy for being her human, indefatigably silly self: a Don Quixote in curls tilting hopelessly but hilariously at the all-too-male establishment.

Lucille Ball's coronation as the First Lady of Television and the high priestess of slapstick began in the 1950s with a six-year run—four in the No. 1 spot. Even after her famous partnership with Desi Arnaz broke up both onscreen and off, audiences continued to love Lucy. Two subsequent Lucy series held down Top-10 ratings for nine years. The secret to her comic genius? "I believe it all the way," she once explained. "I do what I do with all my strength and heart."

Lucy and Lucille, of course, were not the same endearing ditz. Tough, smart, testy and grindingly ambitious, Lucille was a career-obsessed control freak who boasted, "I've never been out of work except for two hours once between contracts." On the set, she monopolized close-ups and demanded star privileges. At home, Ball also played boss, driving her two children like a drill sergeant. But nothing could stop Desi's philandering. Eighteen months after their divorce, Ball married—for keeps—comic Gary Morton. Before her death, she said, "Life is no fun without someone to share it with." ■

"I don't think any public figure—politician or movie star—has ever affected the public like this."
—Carol Burnett

45

FRANK SINATRA

A combustible charmer, he courted the lights, the ladies and trouble

He was clutched by swooning bobby-soxers in '43, dumped by Ava Gardner in '53 (inset, after their '51 wedding) and was still in top form at Radio City Music Hall (right) in '78.

I T'S HARD TO PREDICT WHICH SINATRA WILL HAVE GREATER STAYING POWER: THE Singer, the Swinger or the Scrapper. Following a promising start in 1940 with the Tommy Dorsey band, Sinatra's singing career was sidetracked first by a rapid succession of likable roles on the silver screen, then by a hemorrhage of his vocal cords. But by the late '50s, the Voice was back in front of the mike, interpreting popular songs as no one has done before or since. Master of melancholy, Sinatra burnished his heartthrob image with a number of high-publicity liaisons, as well as marriages to four beauties, among them Ava Gardner and Mia Farrow. Though he was deemed the King of Cool, Ol' Blue Eyes had a fiery temper and alleged Mob connections that left a lash of danger in his ring-a-ding-ding image. ∎

"Frank is the most fascinating man in the world, but don't stick your hand in the cage."
—Tommy Dorsey

ELIZABETH TAYLOR

She upheld our faith in Darwin and survival of the glitteriest

THE BOXING GLOVES BEHIND THE SATIN SLIPPERS." THAT'S HOW photographer Herb Ritts once described Liz Taylor's inner toughness. She has led the kind of bumper-car existence—child star, femme fatale, substance abuser, brain tumor survivor—that causes rubbernecking delays among celebrity watchers. But the public ups and downs have imbued her with a battered grace. "I am living proof of survival," Taylor once said. "I've come through things that would have felled an ox."

The seven husbands tend to overshadow the two Oscars (as the call girl in *Butterfield 8* and the foul-mouthed faculty wife in *Who's Afraid of Virginia Woolf?*). Playing senator's wife was her grimmest, and the two go-rounds with Richard Burton eclipse all other loves. That was pure over-the-top Hollywood. He bought her the 33-carat Krupp diamond as an engagement ring—but would also book hotel suites above and below theirs so nobody could hear those notorious catfights. Yet one of the great enchantresses of the century seems to have found final fulfillment not with another man but as an AIDS activist. "For the first time in my life," she said, "I am making my fame work for me in a positive way." ∎

Taylor, who debuted in film at age 10, has forged an unlikely bond with a fellow early bloomer and tabloid target, Michael Jackson (above, in 1992). In 1969, she and her $1.05-million diamond adorned an Oscar bash with Richard Burton (far right), who had given her the rock.

"She is shy and witty, she is nobody's fool, she is a brilliant actress [and] beautiful beyond the dreams of pornography."
—Richard Burton to his diary

JACQUELINE & JOHN

A dashing couple gave us pause about glamour, money and mortality

IT WAS, IN SOME WAYS, THE Ken and Barbie Presidency: too beautiful to be true. Not to mention too short. Start to finish—from the ringing Inaugural declaration that "the torch has been passed" in Washington in 1961 to the crack of rifle fire in Dallas—John and Jacqueline Kennedy held center stage for just 1,037 days. America's youngest President when he took office and the first Roman Catholic, he died at 46.

But if time and tales of sexual shenanigans have rubbed some sheen off the Kennedy legend, nothing has diminished its power. How else to explain that after Jackie's death her husband's cigar humidor fetched $547,500 at Sotheby's, some 200 times its estimated auction value?

They were the very model of a modern media couple. His

Jackie exuded elegance tending to her daughter or horsing around in '67.

KENNEDY

> "If a free society cannot help the many who are poor, it cannot save the few who are rich." —JFK

on-camera ease in the first televised presidential debates helped him defeat Richard Nixon. Letitia Baldrige, Jackie's social secretary, once tried to explain to the foreign press why the First Lady drew such large, adoring crowds. "Jack Kennedy's our President," Baldrige noted, "but she's our movie star." She was also our style-setter, bringing the arts and a sense of fashion and decor to the public attention. In his opening remarks at an overseas luncheon, the President said, "I am the man who accompanied Jacqueline Kennedy to Paris."

JFK's legacy is mixed and tragically incomplete: on the one hand, there was the Peace Corps, a revived sense of New

51

The family met at Boston's JFK Library in '92.

TOP: REUTERS/CORBIS-BETTMANN; BOTTOM LEFT: IPOL,INC.;RIGHT: HY PESKIN/FPG INTL.

Frontier "vigah" and footprints on the moon; on the other, the Bay of Pigs invasion, the Cuban missile crisis, Vietnam and the Berlin Wall. His First Lady will be treasured for the charm and sophistication she brought to the White House as well as the grace and orchestrating intelligence she displayed in the aftermath of the assassination. "The magic Camelot of John F. Kennedy never existed," concluded historian Theodore White. "But he posed for the first time the question [of that period]. What kind of people are we Americans? What do we want to become?"

Jackie later sought refuge in marriage to the imperious Greek shipping tycoon Aristotle Onassis. After he died in 1975, she applied herself with taste and tact to a new career as a book editor. Through it all, she managed to raise two normal children, calling that accomplishment "the best thing I have ever done." And in the end, as cancer claimed her at 64, she sent out thank-you notes from her deathbed, planned her own funeral, and left her family and her country better for having known her. ∎

Jackie vacationed with Ari Onassis in Greece in '70, left, and gazed at Jack before their '53 nuptials.

"In spite of everything, I still believe people are really good at heart."

JUNE 12, 1929 – MARCH 1945

ANNE FRANK

A lyrical diary spoke of unspeakable crimes and smothered dreams

IN *THE DIARY OF A YOUNG GIRL*, ANNE FRANK PUT A HAUNTINGLY PERSONAL face on the Holocaust. First published in 1947, it has sold more than 25 million copies in 55 languages. From July 1942 until August 1944, Anne and seven family members and friends hid from the Nazis in an attic behind her father's spice factory in Amsterdam. "I see the eight of us as if we were a patch of blue sky surrounded by dark clouds," she wrote. An informant ultimately betrayed them, and only her father, Otto Frank, survived the concentration camp. Anne died of typhus at 15 in 1945 at Bergen-Belsen. A new translation of her diary was published in the U.S. in 1995, replete with the rebellious, coming-of-age musings Otto had edited out of the original. Also released were other writings, including an essay entitled, "Why?" The girl who asked that question would be nearing 70 now. Perhaps an accomplished author. Perhaps an anonymous housewife tending tulips. Regardless, her precocious words had leapt off the page and left us an unforgettable, unfinished symphony of life. ∎

Before the family took refuge, young Anne enjoyed days at a beach near Amsterdam.

BOB DYLAN

Prodded by his caustic visions, the times they began a-changin' faster

WHEN ROBERT ZIMMERMAN GRADUATED FROM HIGH SCHOOL IN 1959, HE announced in the yearbook that he was leaving Hibbing, Minnesota, "to join the band of Little Richard." He never made good on that ambition. But one name change, 30 years, millions of records and multiple musical incarnations later, Bob Dylan did join the "Tutti Frutti" man as one of the early inductees in the Rock and Roll Hall of Fame. Why Dylan, who never met a melody he couldn't strangle? Bruce Springsteen put it well. "Elvis Presley freed your body," he once said. "Bob Dylan—he freed your mind." Indeed, pop music lost its virginity when it met Dylan. His mordant images and stream-of-contentiousness torched moon-june lyric-writing in rock. His attitudes on race, politics, power (the kind that comes from an amplifier) and pot (he turned on the Beatles) challenged, outraged or bewildered his fans even as his oracular style drew more of them. Variously reappearing as a born-again Christian, an Orthodox Jew, a Nashville cat, a recluse, a family man, a shadow of himself, Dylan has been a weather vane even when he's only blowing in the wind. ■

> "I always thought that one man, the lone balladeer with the guitar, could blow an entire army off the stage if he knew what he was doing."

LEFT: ELLIOT LANDY/MAGNUM PHOTOS, INC.; RIGHT: DEBORAH FEINGOLD/OUTLINE

Joan Baez had helped Dylan get started, but he coolly ended their romance during his 1965 tour of England (left).

A former model, Sara Lownds (with Dylan and their son Jesse in 1968) filed for divorce in 1977.

Dylan hit the keys at home in L.A. in 1991, the year the Grammys feted him for Lifetime Achievement.

"Is there a woman who would not want to look like Audrey?"
—Designer Hubert de Givenchy

AUDREY HEPBURN

*Her spritely, style-setting grace
surprised no one but herself*

THERE WERE FLAWS, TO BE SURE, and no one was quicker to point them out than the self-effacing star herself. "Oh, I'd like to be not so flat-chested," Audrey Hepburn once said. "I'd like not to have such angular shoulders, such big feet, such a big nose." Yet the crooked teeth, spritelike ears and impossibly long neck set off a seismic shift that during the '50s converted Hollywood from a zaftig to a slender standard of beauty. "In a cruel and imperfect world," Rex Reed opined upon her death from cancer, "she was living proof that God could still create perfection."

Hepburn's irresistible élan and charm masked a far from perfect private life. An idyllic childhood was disrupted by the split-up of her parents, a Dutch baroness and a British banker. As an adolescent in Nazi-occupied Holland, Hepburn battled hunger and fear as she carried messages for the Resistance in her ballet shoes. Even Hepburn's glory years as a screen goddess were marred by two divorces and multiple miscarriages before the births of her two sons. Yet Hepburn was as indomitable as she was elegant. Upon her retirement, she became a roving ambassador for UNICEF, reaching lives she hadn't already touched by screen. ■

Humphrey Bogart called his *Sabrina* costar (on the set, top right, in 1953) "a delightful elf."

Tirelessly on the road for UNICEF, Hepburn traveled to troubled Ethiopia in 1988.

FEBRUARY 6, 1911 –

RONALD REAGAN

The Gipper went to Washington as the Great Communicator

WHEN RONALD REAGAN FIRST RAN FOR OFFICE, OPPONENT PAT BROWN pooh-poohed his candidacy and Hollywood past. But Reagan's actorly charisma was, in fact, his greatest strength. He unhorsed California Governor Brown by more than a million votes and went on, at 69, to become America's oldest elected President. (He was also the first divorcé, his original marriage having been ended by Jane Wyman, when her acting career eclipsed his.) Somewhat disengaged as an administrator, Reagan preferred to play raconteur-in-chief and national cheerleader, telling us what we yearned to hear: that it was "morning in America" again. But there would be no free breakfast from Reagan, a Republican conservative sworn to end the Soviet "evil empire" and to cut domestic spending. He will be long remembered as a master of the public moment, including his perhaps last, gracefully going public with his diagnosis of Alzheimer's. ∎

"America is too great for small dreams."

MAY 26,1907–JUNE 11,1979

JOHN WAYNE

A Hollywood cowboy romanticized a mythic American West

HE WAS AS UNAMBIGUOUS AS A BELT OF TEQUILA, HIS FAVORITE DRINK. "I don't do much really," John Wayne once said, assaying his career. "Just sell sincerity. And I've been selling the hell out of it ever since I got going." The public obviously bought, establishing him as the most reliable box-office draw in Hollywood history. From 1949 to 1972, he made the movie-house owners' Top 10 list every year but one. Along the way he appeared in some 200 films—including the classics *Stagecoach*, *Red River* and *The Quiet Man*. In or out of the saddle, he played variations on the theme of laconic, straight-shootin' Wild West hero. Wayne called 1969's *True Grit* his one shot at a more dimensional role—a boozy, broken-down federal marshal—and it won him an Oscar.

He was born Marion Morrison, a druggist's son in Winterset, Iowa, and attended the University of Southern California. "I took Latin and mathematics through calculus," he recalled, "and when I started in movies, I had to learn to say 'ain't.' " His drawl and rolling gait were also just tools of the craft ("I practiced in front of the mirror"). He was an icon to fellow conservatives (though he sat out World War II because of an ear ailment) yet appealed across the political spectrum. Picked in a poll as the nation's favorite movie star in 1995–17 years after his death–Wayne stood for (in image, anyway) a bygone frontier spirit that Americans still mourn. ∎

> **"I play John Wayne in every part regardless of the character, and I've been doing okay, haven't I?"**

The Duke chilled on the *Alamo* set in 1959 with his third wife, Pilar, and Aissia, one of his seven kids.

"Guitar groups are on the way out." —Decca Records executive Dick Rowe, rejecting the Beatles following a 1962 audition

THE BEATLES

They led a generation on a magical mystery tour

OR THE YOUTH WHO CAME OF AGE IN BELL-bottoms, long sideburns and love beads, time divides neatly. Before: the stone age that preceded the Beatles' 1964 debut on *The Ed Sullivan Show*. After: the ice age that descended with the 1980 assassination of John Lennon by a deranged fan. And in between? The halcyon era when four clowning lads from Liverpool–John Lennon, Paul McCartney, George Harrison and Ringo Starr–reigned supreme. From "Please, Please Me," their first hit single in 1963, through the release of *Let It Be*, their final album seven years later, the Beatles didn't simply dominate the charts as they racked up 38 gold albums. Benignly, they dictated fashions in clothing, hairstyles, drugs, even spiritual advisers.

Though Lennon and McCartney wrote 20 No. 1 hits together, they couldn't resolve their differences over money, management and mates. After the Beatles split up in 1970, fans' hopes for a reunion faded as each of the Fab Four found a new life. John, who had already formed the avant-garde Plastic Ono Band with wife Yoko, became in the '70s the world's most celebrated house-husband; Paul and wife Linda toured the world with his group Wings, returning to London in 1997 to be knighted; George organized two historic concerts that ultimately raised millions for starving Bangladeshis, then became a movie producer; and Ringo turned up charmingly on children's television. ∎

Their antics in the '64 film *A Hard Day's Night* (left) took a cue from the Marx Brothers, and their beards in '69 mirrored the Maharishi Mahesh Yogi's, but the Beatles were originals.

LEFT: EVERETT COLLECTION RIGHT: GLOBE PHOTOS

> "I am actually not a man of science at all," he said in 1900, before his ideas caught on. "I am nothing but a conquistador by temperament, an adventurer."

SIGMUND FREUD

He excavated the unconscious, and put it on the couch

THESE DAYS, HE IS AS OFTEN DISSED AS DEIFIED, HIS THEORIES as subject to ridicule as reverence. Love him (a case of transference?) or hate him (penis envy, perhaps?), Sigmund Freud was inarguably (a shade defensive, no?) one of the most original and influential thinkers of the 20th century. "Modern man," said Swiss psychiatrist Charles Baudoin, "cannot conceive of himself without Freud." The third of a wool merchant's 10 children, Freud later had six of his own, most famously psychoanalyst Anna. But the Viennese doctor's greatest legacy was his pioneering ideas about the mind, from his theories about "the royal road" to the unconscious (dreams) to his partition of all gall into three parts (id, ego and superego). Inventor of the "talking cure," surely Freud detected more than irony at play when he contracted the mouth cancer that killed him. ■

THE MARX BROTHERS

Riotously ridiculous, they added insult to comedy without injury

THOUGH THEIR FATHER LACKED THE MOXIE TO MAKE IT AS A tailor, the Marx boys' mother had enough ambition for all of her sons. The daughter of vaudevillians, Minnie saw to it that Leonard got piano lessons, Arthur got a harp and Julius got his start on the stage by age 11. Thanks to Mom's chutzpah and the brothers' tenacity, the world got Chico, Harpo and Groucho, the zaniest comic trust of all time. Gleefully irreverent, the Marx Brothers skewered the establishment in 13 films (the first five with brother Herbert, aka Zeppo). Of their behavior on the set, screenwriter S.J. Perelman groused, "They were capricious, tricky beyond endurance, altogether unreliable, and treacherous to a degree that would make Machiavelli absolutely kneel at their feet." And yell, "Hail Freedonia!" ■

Chico: "I would like to say goodbye to your wife."
Groucho: "Who wouldn't?"

Chico, Groucho and Harpo began trouping before World War I and broke up in 1949.

The historic first flight by Orville (right) lasted 12 seconds. By day's end, brother Wilbur had stayed aloft 59 seconds.

As they dared go ever higher, ever faster, ever farther, they fueled our dreams and shattered age-old notions of human limits. Their exploits have expanded our realm beyond the clouds into the heavens

THE WRIGHT BROTHERS

SKY SC

Unfazed by Doubters, Two Shy Bachelors Got Aviation on the Wing

THEIRS WAS A PERFECT COLLABORATION, A SEAMLESS meeting of two sharp minds, two tenacious wills. That rare harmony would prove all the more precious to Wilbur and Orville Wright during the five years that doubt and derision would buffet their claim of having launched the first powered airplane over Kitty Hawk, North Carolina. In Paris, editorialists scoffed, "Flyers or Liars?" In Washington, litigators insisted the achievement had already been claimed by another. Back home in Dayton, Ohio, the local newspaper didn't find the Wright boys' derring-do worthy of mention.

The sons of a pastor who encouraged his five childrens' enthusiasms, the brothers, neither of whom ever married, collaborated from early boyhood. Successively, they made mechanical toys, launched a newspaper on a homemade printing press, built bicycles. When Orville contracted typhoid fever at 25, Wilbur, then 29, distracted his brother by reading news reports of a pioneer glider's death. Soon the Wrights were intent on powered flight. After polishing their pilot skills in hundreds of glider forays, and testing more than 200 wing models in a homebuilt wind tunnel, they constructed *Flyer I*—the plane (with its 12-h.p. engine) they would ride into history on December 17, 1903. That day, each brother made two successful passes. Orville went first because he won the coin toss. Nine years later, typhoid would claim Wilbur, at 45. Orville then sold their patents and tinkered at home until his death at 76, in 1948. ■

RAPERS

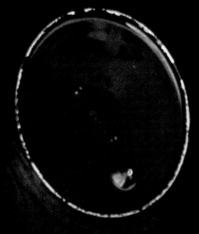

Her Mysterious
Disappearance Has
Made Her Saga the
Holy Grail of Aviation

AMELIA EARHART

When Earhart
wasn't making
history (here,
after her 1935
Hawaii-Califor-
nia flight, a
female first),
she champi-
oned peace and
women's rights.

W HEN AMELIA EARHART, 39, lifted off from Miami on June 1, 1937, no one thought to question what America's favorite aviatrix was up to. After all, this was the Queen of Firsts: first female pilot to fly solo across the Atlantic (1928), first woman to receive the Distinguished Flying Cross (1932), first individual to launch a passenger airline (Boston and Maine Airways, 1933). It made perfect sense that Earhart would want to be the first ever to aeronavigate the globe. Only after Earhart and her twin-engine plane disappeared over the South Pacific—and a 16-day, 4,000-man search produced no traces or clues—did questions begin to percolate.

Sixty years later, authors, documentary makers and expedition buffs are still trying to unravel the riddle of Earhart's disappearance. The standard she-ran-out-of-gas-and-crashed theory has been eclipsed by juicier speculation that the Kansas native was shot down while on a government spying mission. Depending who tells the story, she a) died instantly, b) was executed by the Japanese, c) became the anti-American radio voice of Tokyo Rose, d) bedded down with Emperor Hirohito, e) was relocated by G-men to New Jersey, where she made a life as a homemaker under an assumed name.

No less intriguing are the posthumous assessments of her marriage to George Putnam, the publisher who launched Earhart's career in 1928 by selecting her to be the first woman passenger to fly across the Atlantic. ("I was just baggage," she acknowledged.) Researchers alternately find the Earhart-Putnam alliance: a) a marriage of convenience for both their careers, b) a Svengali-type affair in which he called the shots, c) a modern marriage in which both delighted in manipulating the media. All in all, the woman who claimed she flew simply "for the fun of it" has proved to be, in death more than in life, a) more complex, b) more mysterious, c) more provocative or, actually, d) all of the above. ∎

Earhart and George Putnam (in 1931 after a two-day honeymoon) were pioneers of promotion. To finance her expensive aerohabit, she hawked clothing, cigarettes and luggage.

In Triumph or Tragedy, He Defined Heroism–Not the Other Way Around

After Charles taught wife Anne Morrow to fly, they often traveled together, including this 1931 trip to Asia. Though Anne was a renowned poet and essayist, it was Charles who won a Pulitzer Prize in 1954 for his account of his 1927 flight.

AT THE PEAK OF HIS POPULARITY, HE WAS HAILED AS THE LONE EAGLE, LUCKY Lindy, the Ulysses from Minnesota. At the nadir, he was denounced as an elitist, an isolationist, an anti-Semite. And at various points throughout his nomadic 72 years, he was saluted as a pioneer of aeronautics, medical research and conservationism. But what truly made Charles Lindbergh a cut above your standard-issue American hero was his refusal to be defined or caged by celebrity, notoriety or tragedy.

The only son of an independent-minded U.S. congressman, Lindbergh was raised on an ethic of self-reliance on a Minnesota farm. An indifferent student, he dropped out of college in 1922, his sophomore year, to pursue flying, a passion that had been growing, along with his formidable mechanical abilities, since around age 6. In rapid succession, he offered rides for $5 a head, attended Army flying school, performed air stunts at fairs and flew an airmail route. By 25, he felt ready to tackle aviation's biggest challenge: a solo, nonstop crossing of the Atlantic that carried a prize purse of $25,000. On May 10, 1927, the unknown Lindbergh boarded a plane in New York that he'd christened *The Spirit of St. Louis;* 3,600 miles and 33½ hours later he touched down in Paris, an international sensation.

The resulting hysteria made Lindbergh a millionaire—and a target for the Depres-

CHARLES LINDBERGH

sion-era kidnappings that would soon sweep America. In 1932, the 20-month-old son of Lindbergh and his wife Anne was abducted from their New Jersey home. It took 10 weeks to find the boy's body, two years to arrest a suspect, six weeks to conclude a "trial of the century" that would end with a death sentence (and doubts to this day about the defendant's guilt). Then the media-hounded Lindberghs fled to Europe to reclaim and rebuild their lives. In France, Lindbergh developed a rudimentary artificial heart. In Germany, he acquired an intimate knowledge of the Nazis' air capability.

After the murder of Charles Jr. (above, on his first birthday) the Lindberghs had five more children.

He returned home in 1939 to urge America to remain neutral in the coming European hostilities. After he was branded a defeatist by President Roosevelt in 1941, Lindbergh resigned his Army commission. When he tried to re-up after Japan's attack on Pearl Harbor, he was refused a uniform. Undeterred, Lindbergh flew 50 combat missions as a civilian. Upon his death in 1974, the man who had enjoyed such a mixed reception in the Oval Office—Coolidge awarded him a Congressional Medal of Honor, FDR scorned him, Eisenhower appointed him a brigadier general—was eulogized by President Ford as "a brave, sincere patriot." ∎

Hughes (with copilot) took over the family tool firm at 18, then made movies before switching to aviation.

FPG INTERNATIONAL

He Set Records for More than Oddity

HE'S REMEMBERED AS AN eccentric billionaire whose addictions, idio-syncrasies and mental disorders drove him into seclusion at 45. But Howard Hughes, who died in 1976 at 70, was first a passion-ate flyer. He set speed records for transcontinental and round-the-world flight, designed a plane with a record 319-foot wingspan, founded the Hughes Aircraft Company and built TWA into a world-class passenger carrier. The stars he trekked, though, will always shine less brightly than the ones he dated: Ava Gardner, Jean Harlow, Rita Hay-worth, Katharine Hepburn, Ginger Rogers, Jane Russell. ∎

HOWARD HUGHES

He Flew Around the World in 88 Minutes

Profoundly moved by the assassination of President Kennedy, Glenn quit the space program for politics two years after his historic orbit. His wife, Annie, overcame stut-tering and cam-paigned to help others do the same.

HE FOUGHT IN TWO WARS, flew 149 combat mis-sions, won five Distin-guished Flying Crosses and served four terms as a U.S. sena-tor. But John Glenn Jr., 76, will always be best remembered as the first American to orbit Earth. One of the original Mer-cury Project astronauts, Glenn pierced space on February 20, 1962. When a stabilizing device failed after one swing around the globe, Glenn calmly took over and guided the *Friendship* 7 on its two remaining orbits. ∎

ARCHIVE PHOTOS

UNITED STATES JOHN GLENN Friend7

STEPHEN HAWKING

When Hawking guested on *Star Trek* in '93, Brent Spiner (Data) gasped, "What do you ask the smartest man in the universe?"

From His Wheelchair, He Struts the Cosmos

RAVAGED BY LOU GEHRIG'S disease, Stephen Hawking, 55, is unable to speak or move anything except his eyes and three fingers. But the Cambridge University physicist, widely regarded as the greatest cosmic thinker since Albert Einstein, is attempting nothing less than "a complete understanding of the universe." No one has dared accuse him of hubris. After all, this is the guy whose inscrutable 1988 book *A Brief History of Time* proved the biggest unread bestseller of all time. And the chap who in 1990 dumped his wife of 25 years in favor of his nurse (who was then wed to the engineer who refined his speech apparatus). As Lucy, one of his three children, noted, "He has an amazing capacity to push those around him to the edge of physical and mental collapse, while smiling cheekily to himself." ∎

Her Ecstasy Became The Nation's Agony

NEW HAMPSHIRE HIGH school teacher Christa McAuliffe had just the right stuff to ride Everyman's dreams into space in 1986. Selected from 11,000 private-citizen applicants, she was a 37-year-old wife and mom of two, pretty but not beautiful, fit but not svelte, bright but not brainy. When her "ultimate field trip" with six career astronauts aboard the *Challenger* ended in disaster, an entire nation mourned. ∎

CHRISTA McAULIFFE

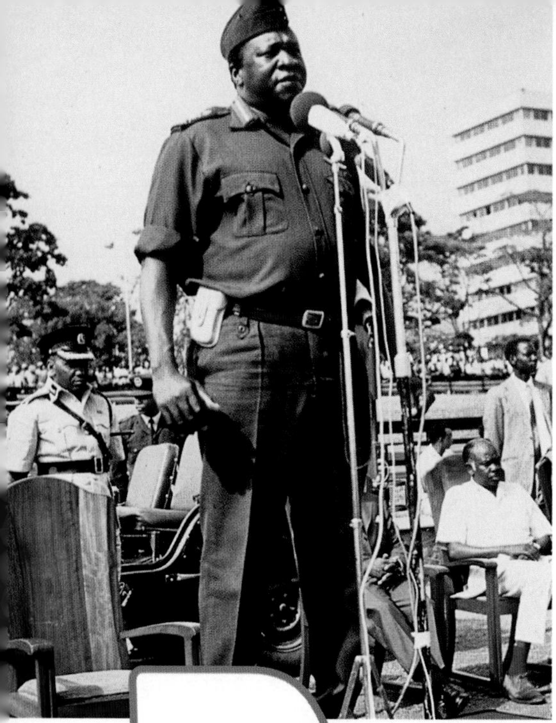

ARCHIVE PHOTOS

Depraved and brutal, they carved up everything from faces and families to peoples and international borders. As they pursued the dictates of their own mad muses, they plunged the world to new depths of horror

Demons and Desp

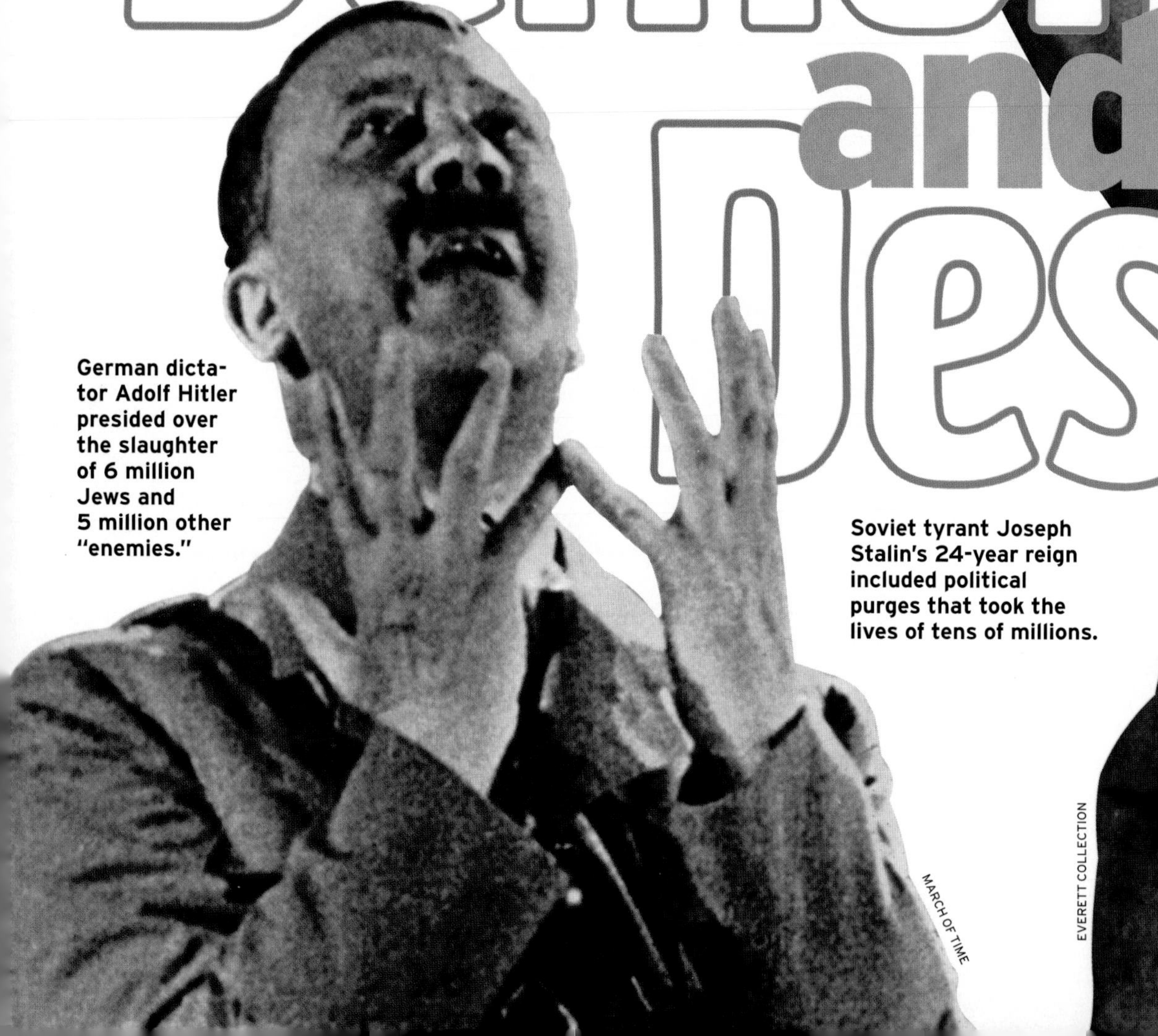

German dictator Adolf Hitler presided over the slaughter of 6 million Jews and 5 million other "enemies."

MARCH OF TIME

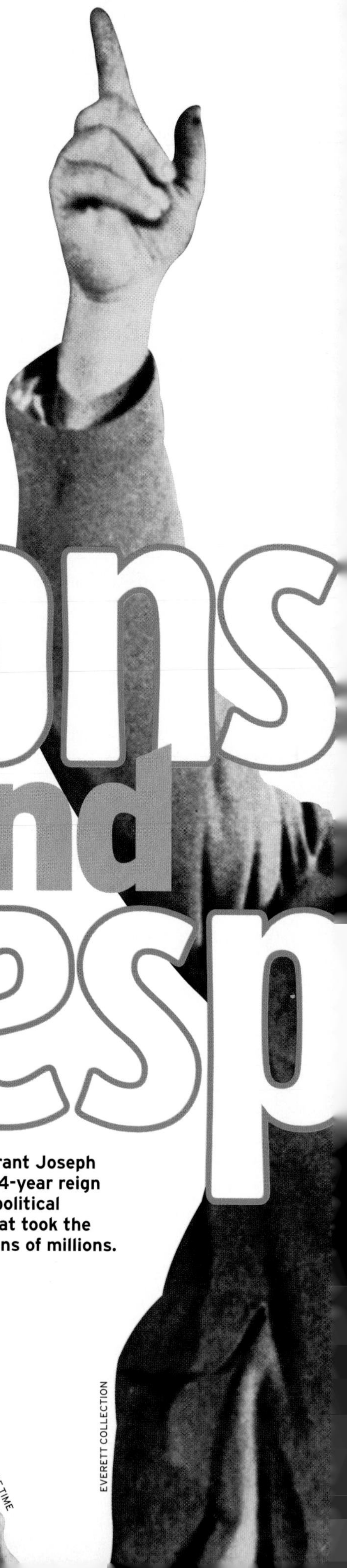

Soviet tyrant Joseph Stalin's 24-year reign included political purges that took the lives of tens of millions.

EVERETT COLLECTION

China's Mao Zedong (above) left a mixed legacy of rapid modernization, a leveling of economic extremes and a body count of 20 to 30 million. By contrast, Uganda's Idi Amin (far left) had only one legacy: the death of some 300,000 countrymen.

ots

HERE WERE DIFFERENCES, TO BE sure. Some butchered on a grand and mechanized scale, in numbers too vast for the mind to comprehend. Others killed intimately, even salaciously, targeting each victim for acts of savagery both imaginative and unimaginable. But whether they terrorized a nation or a city, a lavish encampment or a squalid tenement, the worldview these twisted spirits held was chillingly unambiguous: There was a right way (theirs) and a wrong way (everyone else's). Such clarity of vision made it possible to tear up a nation, tear down a people, tear apart a family, tear off a limb–then go to lunch.

On a sliding scale of horror, it should be easy to rank evils: Just count the bodies. But death is a tricky calculus. In sheer mortal volume, the ruthless ideological campaigns of Mao Zedong and Josef Stalin stand apart. Each resulted in tens of millions of deaths–many deliberate, many more the heedless result of famine, forced labor and relocation. Yet there is no parallel in history for the systematized horror of the Nazi's "Final Solution," a cataclysm that turned 6 million European Jews into hunted animals, stripping them legally and progressively of their rights, their citizenship, their possessions, their humanity and finally their very right to exist.

After Iraq's Saddam Hussein invaded Iran in 1980, 1.5 million died.

Ayatollah Ruhollah Khomeini purged Iran of modernity and liberty.

Violence fed on fear, greed and fantasy

In America, pockets of tyranny thrived. In the '20s and '30s, Al Capone in Chicago (top) and Benjamin "Bugsy" Siegel in New York City made organized crime pay—at least until rivals or the law stepped in. Though hobbled by prosecutions, a stubborn Ku Klux Klan still recruited in '95.

Truth to tell, when the numbers grow too big, we risk feeling—and remembering—too little. Despite pictures of piled skulls seen around the world, it is harder to come to terms with the reality of Pol Pot's "killing fields"—which claimed 3 million Cambodian lives in the 1970s—than it is to be disturbed by a self-generated image of Jeffrey Dahmer excitedly butchering and eating 11 young men because he was "lonely" and didn't want them to leave. The century has had more than its share of grotesque, ritualistic crime—whether Al Capone's 1929 St. Valentine's Day massacre of his rivals, the five senseless murders ordered up by Charles Manson in 1969 or the Ku Klux Klan's hooded terrorism in the 1920s. Perhaps our fascination addresses our deepest fantasies and insulates us from confronting even greater horrors.

Zealots, genocidal murderers and mini-madmen cannot be ranked; they are united mainly by their absolutism. Asked about his persecution of homosexuals, prostitutes and adulterers, Iran's Ayatollah Ruhollah Khomeini explained, "If our finger suffers from gangrene, what do you do? Do you let the whole hand, and then the body, become filled with gangrene, or do you cut the finger off?" Jim Jones, confronted at the eleventh hour by an acolyte who pleaded, "I look at all the babies and I think they deserve to live," answered, "But don't they deserve much more? They deserve peace." What can be said to such people who already have all the answers? ■

Was it a mass suicide or a mass murder that left more than 900 people dead in 1978 at the Peoples Temple in Jonestown, Guyana? A jury took just 17 minutes to conclude that all but two of the deaths at "Jonestown" from cyanide poisoning were the work of cult leader Jim Jones (right) and his henchmen.

The havoc wreaked by psycho killers, though small in scale, was great in impact. The crimes of Jeffrey Dahmer (left, in 1991) revulsed the nation. Fiendish Charles Manson symbolized the flameout of the peace-and-love '60s.

75

Armed only with tenacity and tendentiousness, ingenuity and inspiration, they fought to create a more just world

After the Kings led a five-day march across Alabama in 1965 to protest registration barriers, Congress passed the Voting Rights Act. A year earlier he won the Nobel Peace Prize.

TRAIL BLAZERS

martin luther king jr.

His Was a Dream That Stirred a Nation

MARTIN LUTHER KING JR. HAD OTHER CHOICES IN LIFE THAN TO lead the nonviolent resistance against the bombs of Montgomery, the police dogs of Birmingham and the billy clubs of Selma. When he set off for college at 15, he had hoped to become a doctor or lawyer. He came, after all, from an educated, loving, comfortable Atlanta family that kept him outfitted in his favored tweed suits, and young Martin danced a cool jitterbug and had a winning way with the ladies. Even

BEN MARTIN

after he gained a Ph.D. in theology from Boston University and the hand of Coretta Scott, he still could have chosen an easier path than his lifelong gauntlet of assailants with their rocks and guns, their allegations against his character of infidelity, academic fraud and Uncle Tomism. But King, grandson of the first president of the NAACP and son of an activist pastor, was to the movement born.

Though his life bore no resemblance to that of his sharecropping great-grandparents, King knew the sting of white hatred and black humiliation. When he was 6, the parents of white playmates had sent King packing, reminding him, "You are colored." At 14, he'd been forced to surrender his bus seat to a white passenger and stand the next 90 miles. As a father of four, he'd had to explain to a weeping daughter why her skin color barred her from an amusement park. Yet he refused to be consumed by bitterness, forcefully telling the world in 1963, "I still have a dream." Five years later at 39, America's greatest preacher of nonviolence was in pursuit of that dream when a bullet silenced his sonorous and unforgettable voice. ■

A 1958 arrest for loitering in Montgomery (left) led to one of King's 14 jailings.

King's 325,000 miles of annual travel made family dinners (here in 1965) precious.

TOP: AP; BOTTOM: CAMERA PRESS/RETNA

margaret sanger

Her Life's Crusade Gave Women the Right to Choose

AFFECTED BY HER MOTHER'S EARLY DEATH after having 11 children and seeing a patient die of an abortion in a New York City tenement, a young nurse coined the term birth control and distributed what was, in 1914, illegal information on contraception. Two years later, Margaret Higgins Sanger opened the nation's first family-planning clinic. Though arrested eight times and jailed for a month, she formed in 1921 the organization that became Planned Parenthood, and later supported the development of the pill. She herself had three sons, was married twice and took many lovers, including sex authority Havelock Ellis, before dying at 82 in 1966. Said H.G. Wells: "When the history of our civilization is written, it will be a biological history, and Margaret Sanger will be its heroine." ■

UPI/CORBIS-BETTMANN

babe zaharias

A Jock of All Sports Proved Stardom Isn't for Men Only

AS A KID IN TEXAS, MILDRED DIDRIKSON GOT her nickname bashing home runs like Babe Ruth, and sportswriter Grantland Rice proclaimed her simply "the athletic phenomenon of all time, man or woman." She became a basketball all-American, and set three world track marks (javelin, hurdles, high jump) on her way to two golds at the '32 Olympics. Babe then barnstormed the U.S. playing basketball, baseball and billiards, before settling down to marry 285-pound wrestler George Zaharias and to master golf. She was soon smacking 240-yard tee shots and went on to dominate the women's tour for two decades. Though romantically linked to a competitor on the circuit, she never left her manager-husband. She came back from intestinal cancer surgery with a dramatic win in the 1954 U.S. Open, two years before her death at 45. Upon learning her cancer had returned, Babe said stoically to George, "Well, that's the rub of the greens." ∎

Her 104 points in a high school basketball game were the harbinger of Billie Jean King's 1973 wipeout of tennis chauvinist Bobby Riggs.

margaret bourke-white

A Pioneer Left Us Some of Our Most Memorable Images

AS FAMOUS AND STUNNING AS HER PICTURES, MARGARET BOURKE-WHITE RECORDED the Depression's ravages and World War II for LIFE, and in the '40s snapped Mohandas Gandhi with his spinning wheel and a rare smiling image of Joseph Stalin. Competing in a then-man's business (once, shooting on a yacht, she edged in front of a male news photographer and got pushed overboard), she reluctantly resorted to womanly wiles. "Even Stalin insisted on carrying her bags," noted Alfred Eisenstaedt, a colleague and outspoken admirer of her work. Before she was crippled by Parkinson's disease and died at 67 in 1971, she had two brief marriages, one to novelist Erskine Caldwell. Said biographer Vicki Goldberg: "She was one of a kind, and we should not expect that history will provide the context for another." ∎

betty friedan

Describing 'The Problem That Has No Name,' She Redefined Feminism

WHEN NEWSPAPER REPORTER BETTY FRIEDAN REQUESTED a second maternity leave, she instead got a pink slip. In 1963, Friedan offered her rejoinder, *The Feminine Mystique*, and the American landscape changed forever. Friedan's depiction of the stultifying toll of women's homebound lives—a malaise the "very unbored" Friedan, a suburban mother of three, didn't share—ignited the women's movement, with Friedan (here in '63) at the helm. After the '70s rise of the mythical Superwoman, Friedan bowed out, determined to "reconcile feminism and families." But at 76, her passion has turned to puncturing geriatric stereotypes. With age, she says, "You become more of yourself." ∎

In 1954, Mead used vitamin oil and powdered milk to save this dying baby on a Pacific island.

jane addams

For Immigrants, She Was the Rights-Fighting First Lady

SHE WAS THE STATUE OF LIBERTY INCARNATE, beckoning and backstopping immigrants toward the American dream. From Hull House, the settlement she founded in 1889 in the Chicago slums, Jane Addams crusaded also for labor reform, universal suffrage and other women's issues. Though the daughter of a banker who was a personal chum of Abraham Lincoln, she was no removed limousine liberal but resided herself in Hull House. (Her only marriage was to her causes.) Addams's work with the Woman's International Peace Congress and her pacifism during World War I led to criticism, but Teddy Roosevelt hailed her as "the most useful citizen in America," and four years before she succumbed to cancer at 74, in 1935, she received the Nobel Peace Prize. ■

margaret mead

Intrepid Traveler, She Brought Soul Along with Scholarship

WHEN MARGARET MEAD WAS A CHILD, HER father once lamented, "It's a pity you aren't a boy. You'd have gone far." By the time the anthropologist died in 1978, it was hard to imagine where else she *could* have gone. During her 76 years, she traveled to seven of the planet's remotest recesses to observe primitive cultures, stirring controversy with her multidisciplinary approach to field study and her refusal to remain a mere observer in the face of human suffering. She taught at or received honorary degrees from most of the country's leading universities and presided over several of the scientific community's ranking organizations. She popularized anthropology through her 23 books, hundreds of articles and lectures (as many as 110 a year). And along Mead's peripatetic way (one of her three exes admitted, "I couldn't keep up with her") she pronounced expertly on anything and everything—sexual mores, environmental hazards, race relations, nuclear politics, feminism—earning her the moniker "mother to the world." Jeez, what more did her dad have in mind? ■

In December 1956, Parks legally did what would have been unthinkable a year earlier: took a seat in front of a white passenger on a Montgomery, Alabama, bus. "I had no idea history was being made," she has said. "I was just tired of giving in."

rosa **parks**

An Unlikely Hero, She Refused to Stand for Racism

ON DECEMBER 1, 1955, ROSA PARKS POLITELY REFUSED TO GIVE HER SEAT TO A WHITE man on a Montgomery, Alabama, bus. The 42-year-old seamstress was arrested and fined $14. Despite her husband Raymond's warning ("The white folks will kill you, Rosa"), Parks fought the segregation law in court. The black community—led by a 26-year-old minister named Martin Luther King Jr.—showed its support by boycotting city buses. The protest lasted 381 days, ending when the Supreme Court declared the blacks-in-back ordinance unconstitutional. The civil rights movement was born. King emerged a national figure. But Rosa Parks lost her job and Raymond had a nervous breakdown. They moved to Detroit, where Rosa—now a widow at 84—is a beloved symbol. When she was beaten and robbed in 1994, the police chief fumed, "This is inconceivable. We're talking about a lady who's responsible for changing the course of this country." ■

edward r. murrow

He Gave TV News Its Voice and Conscience

BROADCAST JOURNALISM CAME INTO ITS OWN WITH THE RADIO reports of Ed Murrow from the rooftops of London during the World War II blitz. With peace, his *See It Now* series set the standard for TV documentaries, and one memorable night in 1954 he carved up Senator Joseph McCarthy, hastening the demise of that witch-hunter of alleged Reds. Murrow's tenure at CBS attracted a generation of news giants, including a young wire-service vet named Walter Cronkite. When the chain-smoking Murrow died of lung cancer at 57 in 1965, his old boss Bill Paley described him as "at heart a poet of mankind and, therefore, a great reporter." ■

On *Person to Person* (here in '56), he did live interviews of celebs filmed in their homes.

golda meir

She Helped Give Birth to Israel, Then Nurtured It to Maturity

PERSONALLY SHE WAS SO TENDER SHE WEPT AT the sight of new immigrants, doted on her five grandkids, fussed over Knesset leaders when they assembled in her kitchen for late-night tea and talk. Politically she was so tough that Israel's first prime minister, David Ben-Gurion, called her "the only man in my Cabinet." But from the day Kiev-born schoolteacher Golda Myerson emigrated from Milwaukee to Palestine in 1921, her priority never wavered: to build a Zionist state. During the ascent that led to Meir's 1969 election as Israel's first female prime minister, she put the political before the personal, sacrificing her marriage, suffering a ravaging cancer in silence and reluctantly postponing retirement. The "Mother of Israel" died in 1978 at 80. ∎

Meir (in 1977) was a chosen name that means "light-giver."

WILLIAM KAREL/SYGMA

Robinson (in '45) began his rise with the Montreal Royals, a Dodger farm team.

HAROLD CARTER

jackie robinson

An Electrifying Player Changed Sports History and America

MAJOR LEAGUE BASEBALL CLAIMED TO BE AMERICa's national pastime, but it had no African-Americans until Brooklyn Dodgers general manager Branch Rickey determined to redress the outrage (and to tap the talent-laden Negro Leagues). His careful and, it turned out, ideal choice to lead off was Jackie Robinson, a poised ex-Army officer and four-sport superstar at UCLA. In the face of death threats and catchers who spat on his shoes, this fiery competitor, asked by Rickey to don "an armor of humility," coolly tore up the sport, becoming Rookie of the Year in '47 and making the Hall of Fame. He shared credit with his wife ("When they try to destroy me, it's Rachel who keeps me sane") and wound up a social activist. The eldest of their three kids was a recovering heroin addict killed in a car crash, and Robinson was going to a drug symposium in '72 when he died of a heart attack at 53. ∎

nelson mandela

He Showed South Africa, and the World, a Better Way

On the campaign trail in 1994, Mandela pumped flesh and danced, but his rhetoric was sober, intended less to inspire than to instruct.

HIS TRIBAL NAME, ROLIHLAHLA, MEANS "ONE WHO BRINGS TROUBLE UPON HIMSELF"— and for the longest time, it fit Nelson Mandela aptly. Marked from adolescence as the natural future leader of his Xhosa tribe, Mandela was not afraid of the road less traveled. He nuked his college career by organizing a student strike. He aborted his tribal career by running away at 21 to avoid an arranged marriage. And he destroyed his law career by joining the fight against apartheid. At his 1964 trial for high treason, Mandela risked the death penalty by testifying that freedom "is an ideal I hope to live for and achieve, but it is an ideal for which I am prepared to die." Though the latter seemed more likely during his next 27 years as a prisoner, Mandela refused to be muzzled. From behind bars, he wrote, he inspired, he negotiated. Upon his release, Mandela set out to convince South Africans of all colors that the time had come to make his dream a reality. In 1994 he became his country's first democratically elected president. At 79, Mandela, the legendary troubleshooter, is redesigning South Africa, while Rolihlahla, the twice-divorced trouble-seeker, is pursuing a twilight romance. ■

pope john paul II

With His Global Reach and Personal Touch, He Remade the Papacy

JOHN PAUL II—THE POLISH POPE, AS HE'S AFFECTIONATELY KNOWN—HAS CHANGED THE FACE OF THE PAPA-
cy, the church and the world since assuming the Throne of St. Peter in 1978. The first non-Italian Pope in
456 years, Karol Józef Wojtyla emerged from a communist country, uniquely positioning him to help pry
loose the ironfisted grip of the Soviet bloc. "Everything that happened in Eastern Europe these last few
years," former Soviet leader Mikhail Gorbachev has written, "would have been impossible without the
presence of this Pope." Despite John Paul's rigidly conservative positions on such issues as female priests,
abortion and contraception, he has enjoyed sustained popularity by mixing intellectual rigor and diplomat-
ic sophistication (he speaks seven languages) with an engaging personal warmth and openness. He was the
first Pope ever to attend a Jewish service in a synagogue and the first to use the media effectively to spread
his message. Though at 77 he's in frail health, John Paul remains a vital figure on the world stage. ■

mikhail gorbachev

He Hastened the Demise of the 'Evil Empire'—And His Own Rule

HERE WAS A NOVELTY: A CHARISMATIC, GLAD-HANDing Soviet leader with an engaging smile, a lust to globe-trot and a charming, well-dressed wife. "I like Mr. Gorbachev," British Prime Minister Margaret Thatcher said, three months before Mikhail Gorbachev assumed power in March 1985. "We can do business together." Americans, who affectionately dubbed the preacher of *glasnost* (openness) and *perestroika* (restructuring) "Gorby," embraced his efforts to end the Cold War, decentralize the Soviet economy, mount democratic elections and give citizens a freer voice. So did a Nobel committee, which awarded him the Peace Prize in 1990. But Soviet citizens were less impressed with Gorbachev's "new thinking." They blamed the combine driver's son for unleashing ethnic turmoil and quickening the nation's slide into economic chaos. In December 1991, Gorbachev's "revolution without shots" ended with his voluntary resignation. At 66, he and Raisa, who have one daughter and two grandchildren, often travel abroad, where they enjoy a warmer reception than they do back home. ∎

Before his election as Pope, Karol Wojtyla had been a skiing enthusiast and a canoer with a penchant for alpine hikes. Once installed, he loved to greet his flock (above, in Rome, in 1991).

Devoted companions, the Gorbachevs (in 1986 in what was then East Germany) travel everywhere together. "We are really friends," Raisa once said of her husband. "We have a great complicity."

cesar **chavez**

His Quiet Bravery Sweetened the Grapes of Wrath

Before launching his most famous civil action, the 1968 boycott of California grapes, Chavez helped fuel a *huelga* (strike) in Delano, California, in 1966.

JUST 10 WHEN THE DEPRESSION DEVOURED HIS FAMILY'S 160-ACRE FARM IN ARIZONA, Cesar Chavez spent much of his youth as a migratory laborer, picking carrots and cotton for peanuts. That hardscrabble existence, which rotated him in and out of 65 elementary schools and countless migrants' camps, fueled Chavez's passion "to even the score" for Latinos. His 1965 founding of the United Farm Workers led to improved wages, benefits, educational opportunities and housing for fellow Chicanos, who, upon his death in 1993 at 66, memorialized the ardently nonviolent Chavez as "our Gandhi." ■

malcolm **X**

An Angry Man of the Streets Died a Work-in-Progress

Malcolm X prayed in Cairo during a '64 pilgrimage that opened his eyes to racial harmony. "I feel like a man who has been asleep somewhat," he said, days before his death.

THE KU KLUX KLAN BURNED DOWN HIS HOME IN LANSING, MICHIGAN, HIS PREACHER father was murdered when he was 6, and Malcolm Little wound up a cocaine-sniffing hustler jailed for burglary before he was 21. Then, after embracing the ascetic ways of Islam behind bars and excising his "slave-master" surname, Malcolm X became the strident voice of Black Power in the seething '60s. "We didn't land on Plymouth Rock," he declaimed. "It landed on us." But by 1965, when he was gunned down at 39 by fellow Muslims in Harlem, Malcolm had renounced his racist words and spoke of "all colors coming together as one." Today, as the U.S. drifts toward self-segregation, he is a symbol of prudent separatism, his posthumous *Autobiography* a ringing testament of our troubled times. ■

marian anderson

A Voice of Rare Beauty Soared Above Some Ugly Obstacles

WHEN MARIAN ANDERSON SANG IN AUSTRIA IN 1935, Arturo Toscanini said such a voice "is heard only once in a hundred years." And rarely at that time in her racist native land. Spurned by a hometown Philadelphia music school, she performed mostly overseas and not at the Metropolitan Opera until 1955. Sixteen years earlier, the Daughters of the American Revolution barred her from Washington's Constitution Hall, and Eleanor Roosevelt arranged a concert at the Lincoln Memorial that was called America's first civil rights rally. In a tribute some years before her death at 96 in 1993, black soprano Leontyne Price said, "Because of you, I am." ■

Rudolph Bing belatedly welcomed her to the Met in '55.

PHOTOFEST

Whether draping a frame or framing a shot, dishing out wisdom or whipping up a dish, they set the standard that rivals and wannabes would strive to match

Taste maki

Princess Diana

First, she gave the crusty British monarchy a makeover. Now, she's remaking her life

CLICK: 1981. BEHOLD THE PRINCESS-TO-BE IN THE GIRLISH PINK SWEATER NEStled cozily against her bespoke Prince, her eyes cocked sideward, coy and flirtatious, the tease on her pursed lips a tad shy, a touch triumphant. *Click:* 1981. Behold the new royal highness curtsying before her groom in a dazzling puff of offwhite silk, her gaze direct and luminescent, her lips parted in a smile wide, warm and welcoming. *Click:* 1986. Behold the Princess of Wales in her elegant black dinner dress, one seat removed from her husband, her eyes lifeless and aimed toward the floor, her lips pulled tightly over clenched teeth. *Click*: 1991. Behold the seasoned royal in her stylish dress-for-success peach suit beside her soon-to-be-estranged spouse, hands clasped politely in her lap, her eyes trained skyward, the pinch of her lips radiating tension and

When Diana stepped out to a London charity event in 1994, she exuded assurance. Yet within weeks came reports that she'd been placing bizarre, silent phone calls to an art dealer.

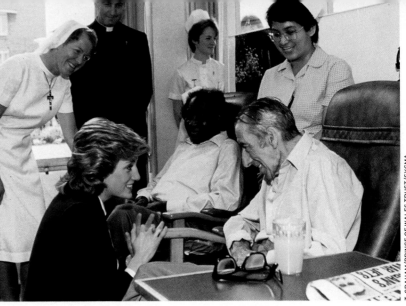

When Diana visited a London hospice in 1985, she demonstrated her free-flowing compassion and easy warmth.

She's tried to shield sons William and Harry (below, in '88) from the flares of her marriage and the glare of public life.

disgust. *Click:* 1994. Behold Princess Diana, her future ex nowhere in sight. Her sporty green jacket is confidently casual. Her mien is delightedly self-assured and glowing.

Never mind that in the early days of her marriage, Diana studied tapes of her public appearances, critiquing every aspect of her presentation like an actress scrutinizing daily rushes for performance flaws. Never mind that behind the fantastic kaleidoscope of clothes, expressions, hairstyles and gestures, Diana always withheld a piece of herself. We think we know her.

We don't. What we know is her natural beauty, her charm and trendsetting sense of style. Her flair for diplomacy and good works. Her plainspoken ease with strangers. And, of course, her well-publicized résumé: Third daughter of an earl. Teenage "Sloan Ranger." Responsible kindergarten aide. Intimidated wife of an inflexible man older in years and higher in station. Doting mother of "an heir and a spare." Depressed and bulimic spouse of a man in love with another woman. Defiant wife with her own cheating heart.

Click: 1997. Behold the mature princess at 35, a $26-million divorce settlement behind, an uncertain future ahead. We don't know Diana. We just wish we did. ∎

Andy Warhol

By cannily celebrating the disposable, he exceeded his own famous 15 minutes

HE "PURSUED FAME WITH THE SINGLE-mindness of a spawning salmon," said one observer. Indeed, Andy Warhol's greatest work of art may have been himself. He predicted that everybody will get 15 minutes in the media spotlight, but Warhol himself wouldn't fade away so quickly. Love him or loathe him, he made an indelible artistic impression, cleverly manipulating mundane images—from Marilyn Monroe's face to Campbell's soup cans—that both exalt and mock the mass culture that produced them. With family roots in Pennsylvania coal country, he was not to the cutting-edge born (though he was hip enough to have three nervous breakdowns as a child). He moved to New York City after Carnegie Tech and became the seminal figure in the Pop Art of the '60s. Warhol made avant-garde films, churned out silk screens by the truckload, edited *Interview* magazine and chronicled snort-on-the-wild-side bohemia. He cultivated an empty-vessel persona, but beneath his bland surface beat a practical heart. "Being good in business is the most fascinating kind of art," said Warhol, who, hours after gall bladder surgery in 1987, died of a heart attack at 58. He left a $500-million estate. ∎

"Art? That's a man's name," said Warhol (with silk-screened Queen Elizabeths in his Manhattan loft in 1986).

Ralph Lauren

Pushing a fantasy of the plush, patrician Good Life put a Bronx boy into the polo set

GERARDO SOMOZA/OUTLINE

His *JE NE SAIS QUOI* WAS EVIDENT BACK IN the 1950s Bronx. "Whatever I had on," he remembered, "other kids would say, 'Hey, where'd you get that?' " Today, the 5'6" former Ralph Lifshitz is an institution, the man who brought pretend aristocracy to America's middle class. In his teens he became a department-store stock boy, then started hustling his own line of overwide ties. Bloomingdale's bought them and, soon, so did everyone else. Today, on his trademark Polo pony, he rides herd on a $2.5-billion clothing and home-design empire and shares four homes with wife Ricky and three kids. All this from a man who wears velvet slippers to work. "Mr. Lauren, is there a particular place you'd like to sit?" a visitor once asked. Yes, he replied. "Wherever the light makes me look best." ■

Her wardrobe (in '41) came from Paris couturiers, but she wore a lab coat in her ads.

EDMUND B GERARD

Helena Rubinstein

A Cracow-born entrepreneur who once studied medicine in Zurich helped change the face of beauty

It was the winter of 1915 when the Polish-born Helena Rubinstein arrived in New York City, and "the women," she noted, "all used dead-white powder. Their lips were gray. Their noses were red from the cold." At her death at 94, five decades later, her salons were correcting that sacrilege with 110 different products. She had carted the original, a skin cream from a Hungarian physician, first to Switzerland (where she briefly attended med school), Australia and then England before invading the States. "Cosmetics merely accent and enhance innate charm and beauty," she preached, "never substitute for it." She was herself 4'10" and built like a cosmetic jar but was a force of (improved upon) nature, marrying twice, the second time to a much younger Russian prince. Along the way, she accumulated $100 million, seven showcase homes, a world-class art collection and a munificent charitable foundation, but was said to sulk over a 50-cent loss in a bridge game. Still driven to the end, the Madame said in her accented English, "I think I've put in 300 years of work in my time." ■

Coco Chanel

She freed women from frills with a certainty as natural as her lines

HE WAS CHRISTENED GABRIELLE BONHEUR (FOR "GOOD FORTUNE") CHANEL, BUT life began grimly enough: a mother dead of tuberculosis and a father who abandoned her when she was 6. Yet in 1922 when Coco (her nickname) introduced what would become her daringly unorthodox scent, she named it Chanel No. 5—because a fortune-teller had once told her it was her lucky number. Aided by a young cavalry officer who turned out to be heir to an industrial fortune (and was one of her many lovers), Chanel reinvented both herself and women's fashion. Among her contributions were clingy jersey knits and the perfect little black dress, as well as bell-bottoms and the classic, boxy suit that still bears her name. The fierce spirit who liberated women from corsets—who made haute couture wearable, even comfortable—never mellowed. In 1969, asked what she thought of 60-year-old Kate Hepburn playing her on Broadway in *Coco*, the 86-year-old grande dame replied, "She's too old." ∎

"From the time I was 12 years old I looked cool," says Lauren (at his spring '95 show). Today, "Ralph's world is not unapproachable or scary," says a competitor. "Everything is done with the promise of good taste."

Chanel (in her studio in 1954) is revered for pioneering the sleek silhouette of modern female attire. "Women are not flowers," she once said of her signature scent. "Why should they want to smell like flowers?"

PAUL HIMMEL/CAMERA PRESS/RETNA

Oprah Winfrey

As materfamilias of TV talk, she presides over the national dialogue

WITH A WARMTH AND VULNERABILITY THAT CAN TAKE THE STING out of the toughest topics, Oprah Winfrey, 43, reigns supreme over TV's daytime gabfest. Five days a week from her Windy City studio, Winfrey enters the homes of 9 million viewers and, mixing celebrity interviews with "real" people panels and self-revealing commentary, helps America hold a mirror to itself. "I don't try to change people," she once explained. "I try to expose them for what they are." Her ever-engaging, never nasty style and her willingness to share details about her personal battles with sexual abuse, weight, fitness and love (she and 10-year beau Stedman Graham, a marketing executive, are still not married) have earned her 25 Emmy awards and made her the world's richest female entertainer. Yet Winfrey remains rooted in the real world, where she mentors kids and champions the homeless in Chicago's slums. ■

Walter Winchell

In the gossip jungle, he was the first big-name hunter, and now everybody's fair game

TALKED . . . AND WROTE . . . LIKE A . . . TELETYPE. But when Winchell dished . . . America listened. From Roaring Twenties . . . to Fabulous Fifties, his news column and radio show . . . scooped the poop . . . on pols and dolls, pugs and thugs. Made 500,000 clams a year . . . in his prime. Started out a New Deal leftie . . . ended up a right-wing cheerleader. Invented power gossip. Yet by his death at 74 in '72, his only son had committed suicide . . . and his two marriages and career had gone (in his own word) "phfft." ■

Johnny Carson

The tube's host with the most brought a touch of legerdemain to late night

HIS PROFESSIONAL DEBUT CAME IN 1939 AT AGE 14: A NEBRASKA ROTARY CLUB PAID "The Great Carsoni" $3 to do magic. Five decades later, Johnny Carson performed a disappearing act before a misty-eyed 50 million viewers, surrendering his *Tonight Show* sword with characteristic grace after a three-decade run. "The move was right," he later said. "The timing was perfect." His timing was *always* perfect. Carson's mastery of the monologue and what a critic termed "ageless agility" were unequaled in the so-called cool medium. After retiring, he swatted tennis balls at his Malibu home and hopscotched around the world with his fourth wife, Alexis. Now 71, he has admitted favoring the Discovery Channel over Dave, Jay or Conan. Who can blame him? Everyone else is a pretender to his throne. The audience has splintered. The communal thrill is gone. "More people look at Johnny," an NBC flack once said, "than look at the moon." No more. The moon is still there. But there's a gaping hole in late-night TV. Said Milton Berle: "What he did was a miracle." ■

Carson (in '85) invited Bette Midler on his penultimate night in '92, and she sang "You Made Me Love You," with new lyrics just for him.

GLOBE PHOTOS

BOB D'AMICO/OUTLINE

Vince Lombardi

The lord of discipline helped launch a new Sunday religion

BEFORE "TOUGH LOVE," THERE WAS LOMBARDI. THE CLENCH-JAWED coach led his Green Bay Packers to five NFL titles, plus victories in Super Bowls I and II in '67 and '68. Reared in Brooklyn, he had contemplated becoming a priest, but opted for preaching a color-blind, be-all-that-you-can-be work ethic that welded athletes into true teams. ("Coach Lombardi treats us all alike," one Packer memorably moaned. "Like dogs.") Lombardi didn't like long hair. Or sports agents. But players revered him and he became the Babe Ruth of football, even though he starred from the sidelines: that rare personality who captures the spirit of his sport and drives it to a new level of popularity. Which is why the winner of every Super Bowl takes home the Vince Lombardi Trophy. ∎

"I wish to hell I never said the damn thing," Lombardi (in the late '60s) once groused about his oft-quoted maxim ("Winning isn't everything. It's the only thing."). "I meant the total effort. . . . I meant having a goal."

Bill Gates

The nerd whose software transformed the digital world now virtually owns it

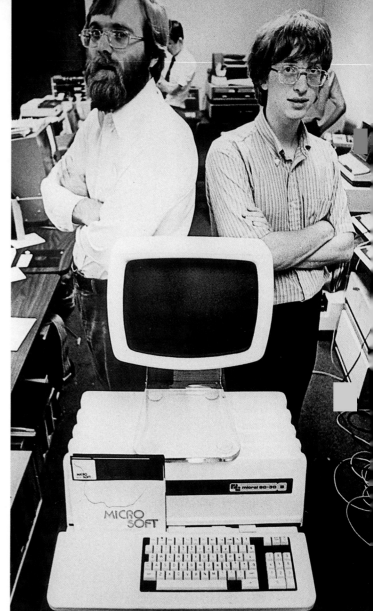

WHO SAYS GARBAGE IN, GARBAGE OUT? Bill Gates and childhood pal Paul Allen launched themselves raiding the trash cans of a Seattle computer company. "I'd get the notes out with coffee grounds on them and study the operating system," recounts Gates. By high school, he was earning $20,000 as a programmer. He did get into Harvard but dropped out to form Microsoft Corporation with Allen in 1975, and together they designed the breakthrough software to run the first microcomputers. Some $24 billion later, Gates is the world's richest man, with Microsoft software humming inside 85 percent of the world's hardware. In one six-year stretch in the supercompetitive field, he took only six days off but has mellowed since an office romance with one of his execs, Melinda French, led to marriage and then added Jennifer, 1, to their network. Having built himself a 40,000 square-foot, $40 million-plus house, he still has loftier dreams than creating computer chess champs. "I don't think there's anything unique about human intelligence," he has said. "We can someday replicate that on a machine." ∎

"I don't plan to retire to some deserted island," says Gates, 41 (with Paul Allen, left, in '81). "I wouldn't meet smart people."

Benjamin Spock

A gentle doctor delivered a new way of child rearing

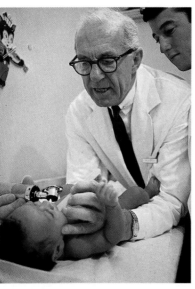

ONLY THE BIBLE HAS OUT-SOLD *BABY AND CHILD CARE*, STILL in print after 52 years and 40 million copies. Dr. Spock, now 94 and chilling out in Maine, turned the stern, old-school parenting he got in Connecticut on its ear. Hugs and psyche-soothing were in, belt-buckle discipline out. Conservatives consider Spock, an anti-Vietnam activist, the godfather of permissiveness. But his latest book, *A Better World for Our Children*, written after his divorce and difficulties raising a stepchild (he was 72, she 11), scolded a society rife with violence, materialism and "coarsening" sexual attitudes. "When I think of the millions of children exposed every day to its harmful effects," he wrote, "I am near despair." ∎

Roseanne

She enthroned herself as the gonzo goddess of blue-collar comedy

HE WAS A TRAILER-DWELLING COCKTAIL WAITRESS TURNED TV'S MOST UNBRI-dled producer-star—think of Lucy, with a Uzi. "I want this show to tell the horri-ble truth," she proclaimed, and *Roseanne*, which just ended its nine-year run, delivered, providing a needed jolt of reality comedy, grounded in lower-middle-class angst and a kind of Wal-Mart feminism. It also brought to center stage Roseanne's mon-strous ego, with her public charges that she was abused by both parents, flashing his-and-hers butt tattoos, not to mention her butchering of the national anthem and two ex-husbands. "I'm only upset," she declared on MTV of her '94 bust-up with Tom Arnold, "that I'm not a widow." Roseanne, now 44, aims to sit back and create programs, including her own talk show in 1998, that, no surprise, "empower women." ∎

"I'm proud to be a working-class person," she said (above, in '87). "That's who I want to be and talk to."

Jane Fonda & Ted Turner

Having burned buns and bridges for years, they can't stop smokin'

HE GAVE THE WORLD NEWS ON DEMAND. SHE GAVE THE WORLD FITNESS ON demand. And since their marriage in 1991, the seemingly inseparable dynamo duo of Ted Turner and Jane Fonda have given each other mutual support on demand. Alternately revered and reviled, Turner and Fonda have affected lives the world over. In 1980, Turner revolutionized journalism with his launch of the Cable News Network, making up-to-the-instant news available to international audiences round-the-clock. Fonda, meanwhile, ignited a fitness revolution with the 1982 release of the first of her 23 hot-selling exercise videos.

At 58, Turner has expanded into movie, sports, cartoon and business channels and merged with Time Warner. Fonda, 59, has moved on from Broadway ingenue, screen sex kitten, political activist, serious actress and producer to superspouse. "Ted Turner is not a man that you leave to go on location," Fonda once explained. "He needs you there all the time." ∎

Fonda (right, in '88) and Turner (with Jane in '90) share more than a passion for outdoor sports, the environment and the Atlanta Braves. Each had difficult, demanding fathers, a parent who committed suicide and two broken marriages.

Stephen King

The master of disaster gleefully brought gothic gore to a suburban setting

EVERETT COLLECTION

IN THE RIGHT HANDS, DUST BALLS UNDER A BED can be terrifying objects. Those hands, of course, belong to Stephen King. The guitar-playing, motorcycle-riding shock trooper from Maine has been churning out spine-chillers for more than 20 years. Tales of killer dogs *(Cujo)*, haunted hotels *(The Shining)* and telekinetic prom queens *(Carrie)*: 40-plus books, more than 150 million copies.

King wrote his first story at 7, sold his first at 18. The source of his demon imagination? Could be Dad ditching the family when King was 2, although he credits the Methodist church: "The horror stories I grew up on were biblical stories . . . the best horror stories ever written." Critics yawn, but King took the gothic novel mainstream. Sci-fi writer Orson Scott Card says ultimately he'll be "regarded as the dominant literary figure of the time." But critics don't scare King. At 49, he enjoys life with his wife and three kids, and cranks out six creepy pages a day. "There's a lot of mystery in the world," he says, "a lot of dark, shadowy corners we haven't explored yet." ∎

"I just want to scare people," says King (in '92). "I'm very humble about that."

Steven Spielberg

He's the ultimate special-effects man: Every movie he touches turns into gold

STEVEN SPIELBERG'S GRADES WERE SO BAD HE COULDN'T GET INTO COLLEGE FILM school, but he went on to create four of the top 10 moneymakers of all time: *Jaws, E.T., Indiana Jones and the Last Crusade* and the worldwide numero uno, *Jurassic Park.* A likely billionaire even before its sequel this year, he is, at 50, a cofounder of the heralded DreamWorks studio.

Growing up with parents who migrated from New Jersey to California and eventually divorced, he says, "I responded by escaping into my imagination." With the 8-mm

camera of his electrical engineer dad, he had filmed a precocious, 40-minute war flick by the time he was 13. But until 1994, the critical rap on Spielberg was that he had a knack for charming if mindless blockbusters. That year came *Schindler's List.* The following spring, he had his bald spot sprayed black for Oscar night and won for Best Picture and Director of the brooding tale of the Holocaust. George Lucas, no slouch himself *(Star Wars)*, compares his co-worker to "Einstein or Babe Ruth or Tiger Woods. He's not in a group of filmmakers his age; he's far, far away." ∎

Spielberg—directing *Jurassic Park* (left in '93) and and on *The Color Purple* location in '85 with Whoopi Goldberg—has a box-office head start with a brood of seven: a child with first wife Amy Irving, and five with Kate Capshaw plus one of hers.

"I had to change— or die," Ford (on the '76 campaign trail) once said of her dependence on alcohol and painkillers.

Betty Ford

Candid and courageous, she led the way in bringing recovery out of the closet

IN AUGUST 1974, SMILING WANLY IN HER POW-der-blue suit, she held the Bible as hubby Jerry was sworn into office. Lying awake that night she thought, "My God, what a job I have." The U.S.'s 35th First Lady, a onetime Martha Graham dancer and fashion model, rose valiantly to the challenge. In September of that year she learned she had breast cancer, and her public, post-mastectomy candor forced women—literally—to learn to examine themselves. In 1978 came an even bigger bombshell: that the ex-President's wife, after family intervention, had admitted a secret addiction to vodka and pills. Today, at 79, she has built a living monument to modern enlightenment: her namesake 80-bed clinic in Rancho Mirage, California. Addiction, Betty Ford has helped teach us, is "a disease, not a crime." ■

Walt Disney

When he wished upon a mouse, he made America's dreams of innocence come true

AS A BOY IN RURAL MISSOURI, WALT DISNEY drew sketches of farm animals for the town barber in exchange for haircuts. That abili-ty to blend art and commerce flowered when he moved to Hollywood in 1923 and opened a cartoon studio with older brother Roy. Five years later, the animated short *Steamboat Willie* (with Walt pro-viding the squeaky voice of his creation, Mickey Mouse) launched their fantasy factory. Soon came Hollywood's first feature-length cartoon (*Snow White and the Seven Dwarfs*), later the Mouse-keteers, Disneyland and the live-action *Mary Pop-pins*. Critics derided the Disney empire as escapist fluff. Walt (a lifelong smoker who succumbed to lung cancer at 65) saw it differently. "We're selling corn," he admitted. "And I like corn." ■

"I guess I'm an optimist," said Disney (in '53). "I'm not in business to make unhappy pictures."

Kroc, tasting success in '75, was 52 when he "decided to go for broke."

VINCE STREANO

Ray Kroc

A burgermeister struck it rich by putting convenience on a bun

RAY KROC KNEW: GRILL IT AND THEY will come. A high school dropout, he'd been a jazz pianist, paper-cup salesman and milk-shake machine distributor when he stopped by an assembly-line burger joint in San Bernadino, California, run by a couple of brothers named McDonald. Kroc negotiated franchise rights and a year later, in 1955, opened the first spinoff outside Chicago. Timing was perfect: The suburbs were booming, teenage labor was plentiful and America had lost interest in home cooking. Kroc's fanaticism about cleanliness and details didn't hurt. *Every* burger had to be .221 inches thick and 3.875 inches wide; and he often personally scouted new locations and managers. Kroc also refused to hire girls (saying they attract the "wrong kind" of boys) until a federal job-discrimination law was passed. His golden-arches touch failed only with a flyer into a business less subject to quality control—the San Diego Padres. "There's a lot more future," he discovered, "in hamburgers than in baseball." When he died in 1984 at 81, the fast-food revolutionary was worth $500 million. ∎

Martha Stewart

Her fanatical yet seemingly effortless pursuit of the exquisite has everyone trying to keep up

EITHER YOU GET MARTHA STEWART OR YOU don't. Many obviously do. It's not just the 2 million people who read her award-winning bimonthly, *Martha Stewart Living*, to savor her tips on everything from arranging flowers, photographs and dinner parties to refurbishing furniture, pools and houses. Stewart, 55, also has huge audiences for her 18 books, her syndicated TV show and newspaper column, her thriving video and mail-order products. This former model and stockbroker—who grew up in Nutley, New Jersey, in a Roman Catholic, Polish-American family—doesn't merely rinse chickens; she shampoos them. The Stewart style began in 1972 when she and her publishing exec husband (they split in 1987) bought a fixer-upper in Westport, Connecticut. That house became the 1980 launchpad of Martha Stewart, Inc., which has since grown into a $200-million empire. To her critics, she says, "I'm only trying to make people's lives a little more pleasing to them." ∎

Stewart (in 1995) has one child, two houses and "not enough time in the day."

STEWART FEREBEE/OUTLINE

Julia Child

Part chef, part comedienne, she translated French cooking for the American masses

INGREDIENT FOR INGREDIENT, IT HARDLY SOUNDED LIKE A RECIPE FOR RATINGS. Take one unpredictable, prank-prone woman, drape her 6'2" frame in a blue apron, mike her foghorn voice, then turn her madcap energy loose before a TV camera. *Et, voilà!* Sheer culinary, comedic magic. Since the 1963 launch of *The French Chef* on PBS, Julia Child has become as much a kitchen staple as a whisk. Her first pioneering series, which ran 11 years and continues to air in reruns, launched a French revolution in the American kitchen. Her secret? Good ingredients. Hard work. And a practical streak that can reassure even the most inept chef. "Remember," she exhorted her audience after dropping a potato pancake on the floor, "you are alone in the kitchen." Actually, though, it was the other presence in her own kitchen, first in France, then in Massachussetts, who most inspired the native Californian's cooking: Paul Child, her beloved diplomat husband of 48 years, whom she once described as "a hungry man interested in food." At 84, the indefatigable Child is relishing her fourth PBS series, *Baking with Julia.* ∎

As the U.S.'s favorite French chef (here, in 1966), Child aimed to "take the mystery and the folderol ouf of French cooking." Even a radical mastectomy and her husband's death in 1994 haven't deterred Child from her mission.

NBA great Larry
Bird once
mused, "Maybe
the guy is God
disguised as
Michael Jordan."

Michael Jordan

All hail the basketball player from another planet

A CHICAGO BULLS ROOKIE, B.J. ARMSTRONG, ONCE READ A
book about Einstein and Mozart in hopes of fathoming the
genius of teammate Michael Jordan. Why bother? Just enjoy.
Driving, soaring, his tongue flapping like a commuter's tie, Jordan is
free verse in motion, peerless on offense, relentless on defense, tireless in practice. And irresistible, whether charming or chiseled, as a
pitchman for Nike, McDonald's and Gatorade. "I would like to be able
to do normal things," Jordan has said, meaning spend more time with
his wife and three kids or strolling a golf course. Hoodlums robbed
him of his beloved father on a North Carolina roadside, but nothing
can take away Jordan's love for the game or for living to the max. ∎

Nadia Comaneci

With poise beyond her years, she earned a string of 10s and ignited a gymnastics craze

I N THE WORLD OF ELITE GYMNASTICS, WHERE A judge's perception of a bobble can prove ruinous, all gold may glitter, but it doesn't all have the same sheen. Rare is the champion who all can agree was indisputably the best. Such an Olympian was Nadia Comaneci, who at 14 won both hearts and medals at the Montreal Summer Games. Her historic string of seven 10s in '76 built on the interest ignited four years earlier by charismatic Soviet gymnast Olga Korbut, inspiring tykes the world over to take up the sport, a prepubescent rage that has yet to fade. Comaneci continued to make headlines as she successively defected from Romania, and battled damaging rumors of bulimia and an affair with a married man. Then, in a fairy-tale moment, she married American gymnast Bart Conner, and now works with him at his gymnastics school in Oklahoma. To her fans, though, she'll always be as she was when she captured the world's first 10. Spritely. Mysterious. Perfect. ■

Tiger Woods

Roll over, Arnold Palmer, and tell Jack Nicklaus the news: Supergolfer is here

T ALK ABOUT HEAD STARTS. TIGER Woods was a regular at a Cypress, California, driving range at 18 months, wheeled in a stroller by his mom, Kultida. With less sensitive nurturing he could have turned out a Tonya Harding. But now, in his first year as a pro, the 21-year-old phenom has won the legendary Masters, collected $1 million in prize money faster than anybody in history (nine tourneys vs. the old record of 28), and inked $60 million-plus in endorsements. Woods's father, Earl, is African-American and a retired Green Beret lieutenant colonel; his mother is Thai. With his silky swing and sincere smile, Tiger is thus poised to become an ambassador of diversity in a largely lily-white sport. He says he wants "to help kids in the inner city play golf." But Earl believes "the Almighty" has a plan in mind for his son that will "make an impact on the world." Hmmm. A middling actor became President. Why not a great golfer? ■

A Daddy's Boy, Tiger took up golf "to emulate the person I looked up to more than anyone: my father."

MARILYN *Monroe*

THE S*ex*

Beauty she had aplenty (in 1959, right), but in 1953's *Gentlemen Prefer Blondes* (left), she proved her comic talent as well.

Hot or Not, She Just Wanted to Be Liked

THERE ARE THOSE, LIKE JEAN HAR-low, who came before, and those, like Madonna, who came after. But of the many aspirants to that deification most revered and reviled in the cultural pantheon, the sex goddess, none sits higher than Marilyn Monroe. Sultrily silken yet winsomely wholesome, maddeningly unattainable yet touchingly human, Monroe was the breathless blonde temptress who could tantalize without intimidating. "For the entire world," her acting teacher Lee Strasberg eulogized at her 1962 funeral, "she became a symbol of the eternal feminine."

That was in life. In death, the Monroe myth grows only larger as every moment of her 36 years is revisited,

To Norman Mailer, this basking former calendar model (here in '49) was the "Stradivarius of sex."

With messages that variously teased, titillated and taught, these pinups, hunks and love doctors liberated sex from the Victorian closet, enabling us to acknowledge this most primal of human instincts in all its manifestations

iest CENTURY

TOP LEFT: EVERETT COLLECTION; PELE/STILLS/RETNA, LTD. (2)

reinterpreted, reinvented. Indeed, there have already been more than 50 books. Psychologists scavenge around her Los Angeles childhood, probing family patterns of mental illness and Monroe's turbulent rotation through 12 foster homes before age 16, when she married for the first of three times. Recovery gurus peer through the haze of Monroe's alcohol and pill habits to retrace the zigs and zags of her 29-film career and her failed marriages to baseball great Joe DiMaggio and celebrated playwright Arthur Miller. Gossip writers reimagine Camelot, placing Monroe between the sheets with the brothers Kennedy, John and Robert. And conspiracy buffs festoon her deathbed with tendrils leading from the killer bottle of barbituates to the White House, Cuba or the Mob.

Did Monroe suffer from the same mental illness that repeatedly hospitalized her unmarried mother? Was she raped by one of her many foster parents? Was her alleged suicide actually an accidental, depression-induced overdose or a murder? As new fact and fiction perenially rekindle Monroe's incendiary mix of heart-stopping beauty, heart-pounding sensuality and heartbreaking vulnerability, the sex goddess is proving a true immortal. ■

Monroe's hooded gaze (above left) often bespoke pills and booze.

She met with hubby Arthur Miller (left) and Laurence Olivier in '57.

Her earlier marriage to Joe DiMaggio (below) lasted only nine months.

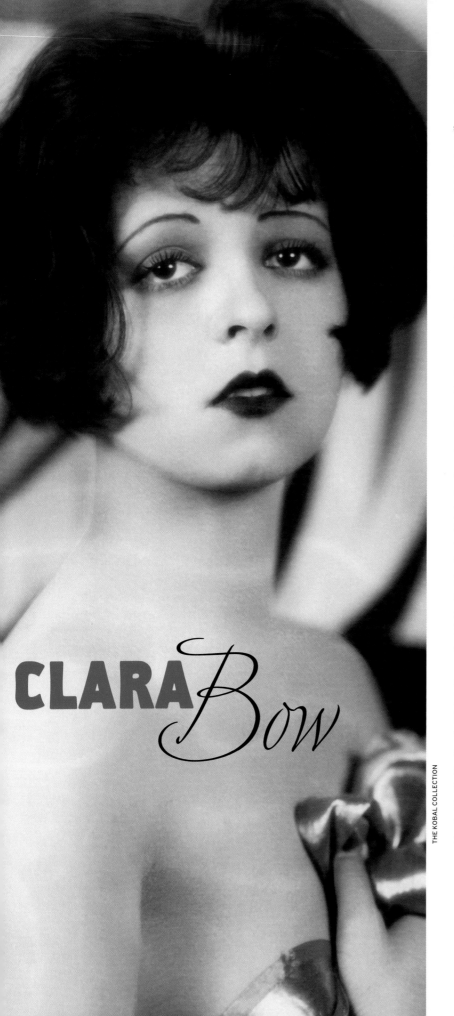

CLARA *Bow*

THE KOBAL COLLECTION

The 'It' Girl Proved Too Wild for Her Time

WITH HER FULL-MOON EYES, Kewpie-doll lips, flame-red hair and hoydenish air, Clara Bow became Hollywood's first sexpot, or as she was known in the Jazz Age she personified, the "It" Girl. F. Scott Fitzgerald wrote one of her early films, *Grit*, in 1924, and the frantic following year she appeared in no less than 14, with lurid titles like *The Primrose Path* and *The Scarlet West*. In 1927 came *It*, during which she had an off-set fling with a young Gary Cooper, a flagrant habit that helped derail her career and life.

Bow had escaped at 16 from a battered childhood to a beauty contest that won her a movie cameo. Unlike many of her peers and despite her Brooklyn accent, Bow made the transition to talkies. But by the 1930s it was all but over amid press outrage and studio jitters after a succession of scandalous romances, gambling debts, bounced checks, blackmail and drug charges.

Of all her men, Bow married only one, a B-movie cowboy, Rex Bell, and moved to Nevada. She briefly emerged from mental troubles and obscurity in 1960, declaring to Hedda Hopper, "I slip my old crown of 'It' Girl not to Taylor or Bardot but to Monroe." Five years later, the original titleholder died in Hollywood, a recluse at 60. ■

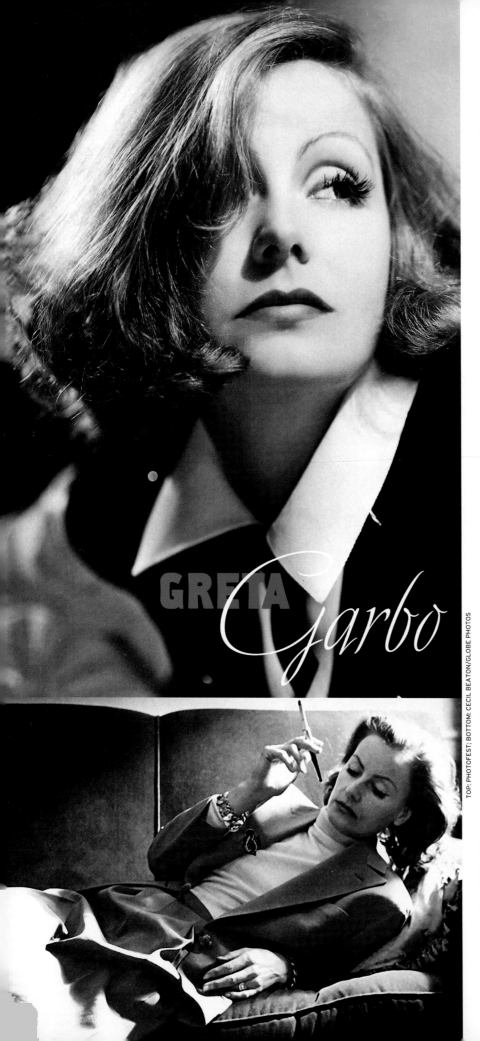

GRETA *Garbo*

TOP: PHOTOFEST; BOTTOM: CECIL BEATON/GLOBE PHOTOS

More Than Fame, She Coveted Privacy

EXOTIC, ENIGMATIC, AS ICILY cool onscreen as she was scorchingly tragic, Greta Garbo had the allure of the unattainable. Whether performing for the camera or ducking it, her message was the same: She wanted to be alone.

Garbo began life in a shabby district of Stockholm, where she quit school at 13 to care for her ailing father, an unskilled laborer. When he died a year later, she became a latherer in a barbershop, then landed a spot in a promotional film that led to an acting scholarship. By 20, Garbo was in Hollywood, where she made 24 films. Her transition to talkies was trumpeted with the pitch, "Garbo Talks!" but the real Garbo was so aloof that she sometimes barred even directors from her set. "When people are watching," she said, "I'm just a woman making faces for the camera. It destroys the illusion." At 36, the "Swedish sphinx" quit the screen and embarked on a Manhattan life of much walking and little talking. Beyond her jilting of silent-movie hunk John Gilbert in 1926 on what was to have been their wedding day, little is known about Garbo's liaisons. When she died at 84, the cause was, like her life, a mystery. ■

At her peak (above, in 1933), Garbo was celebrated by critics as "every man's fantasy mistress."

Despite her retreat into seclusion (left, in 1946), she said, "You know, I've led a fabulous life."

ERROL *Flynn*

A Celluloid Swordsman, He Put World Womankind on Guard

HE WAS BORN DOWN UNDER AND LIVED over-the-top. Errol Flynn, who boasted that he'd "seen everything twice," worked his way around the world as a sailor, newspaperman, plantation overseer and, according to one unlikely biography, Nazi spy. Flynn's true calling was film, in which he was at his dashing, devil-may-care best in period pieces like *Captain Blood* and *The Adventures of Robin Hood.* Bette Davis, his costar in *The Sisters,* called him "handsome, arrogant and utterly enchanting." Jack Warner, preeminent of the moviemaking brothers, found Flynn mediocre as an actor but magnetic. "He was," Warner summed up, "one of the most charming and tragic men I have known." A rape trial involving two teenagers soiled Flynn's reputation even though he was acquitted. Typically he met his second wife in the courthouse, and when he died in 1959—a boozed-up, burned-out 50-year-old party boy—he was keeping company with a teenage actress. Yet Flynn's attraction seemed indestructible. As the third of his three ex-wives said, "I wish I could hate him, but I can't. He's the most lovable man in the world." ∎

Flynn made a swashbuckling point in a 1936 PR shot. Unapologetic about his prodigal life, he once said, "Any man who dies with more than $1.05 [unspent] is a jerk."

She Loved to Flirt Primarily with Propriety

DURING WORLD WAR II MILITARY MEN REFERRED TO THEIR INFLAT-able life jackets as Mae Wests. Such was the cultural impact of the mistress of innuendo. "I take sex out in the open and laugh at it," said West. She was a vaudeville vet (her one brief marriage was to a song-and-dance man) who made a splash in 1926, drawing 10 days in jail for writing and starring in a risqué Broadway play titled *Sex*. A few years later she took her saucy saloon-girl act to Hollywood, providing an early starring role for Cary Grant in *I'm No Angel*. Dozens of coolly delivered, self-scripted lines ("Is that a gun in your pocket, or are you just glad to see me?") prompted censorship rules that lasted until the 1960s. Two years before she died following a stroke at 87, West was still vamping and camping in the movie *Sextette*. ∎

MAE *West*

In her own shrewd self-appraisal, she was "a sex personality not a sex symbol."

Was Paris Burning? Oui, After She Arrived

WHEN JOSEPHINE BAKER MADE HER PARIS DEBUT PERFORMING HER erotic "Danse Sauvage" nude except for flamingo feathers, *toute* France was instantly turned on to black beauty and "le jazz hot." By the age of 20, she had risen from the slums of St. Louis (not *Ile de* but Missouri) to Harlem to running her own Parisian boîte and walking her pet leopards down the Champs-Elysées. Happy as an expatriate, she returned to the States in 1963 to march and perform for civil rights, and her World War II service with the French Resistance won her the Croix de Guerre. Though she wed twice before dying of a stroke at 68, the love of Baker's life was her adopted brood of 12 multi-racial children. She dubbed them her "Rainbow Tribe." ■

Called by Colette "the most beautiful of panthers," she found in exile her natural habitat. "I wanted to find freedom," she said, "[and] I couldn't find it in St. Louis, of course."

ROGER VIOLLET/LIAISON NETWORK

JOSEPHINE *Baker*

RUDOLPH *Valentino*

ARCHIVE PHOTOS/AMERICAN STOCK

He Kissed the Girls And Made Them Sigh

"THE BIGGEST THING VALENTI-no did was to die," said one of his leading ladies. Indeed, when the hot-lipped star succumbed at 31 to peritonitis, a cult was born. Police had to beat back frenzied women at his funeral—and several committed suicide. An Italian émigré, he had toiled as a dishwasher, gigolo and petty thief before the comet-like film career that ended in 1926 with *Son of the Sheik* (costarring Vilma Banky, left). The great romantic idol of the silents did live long enough to have two failed marriages, both to lesbians. ■

PAUL NEWMAN & JOANNE WOODWARD

Their Love Remains a Long Hot Summer

I THOUGHT, 'JEEZ, WHAT A PRETty girl,' " Paul Newman said of first spotting Joanne Woodward in 1953 in New York City. She remembered it differently: "I hated him on sight." But they wed after making *The Long Hot Summer* in 1958. Bliss? Not always. The strains of a one-sexsymbol, two-career and threechild family have occasionally roiled the waters in their Connecticut home. Now, though, he's 72, she's 67, they've become grandparents and they enthusiastically support each other's separate projects. "Joanne genuinely thinks he's delightful," says colleague James Naughton. "And he seems to delight in her." ∎

BRUCE DAVIDSON/MAGNUM PHOTOS, INC.

They Were the Silver Screen's Golden Pair

WHEN THEY MET IN 1936, RUGGED Clark Gable, 35, whose second marriage was foundering, was called the King in Hollywood, and the divorced Carole Lombard, 28, was the sassy queen of romantic comedy. For six idyllic years (they wed in '39 and lived in a restored farmhouse in California), "they were soulmates who thought life was delicious," recalls friend Esther Williams. But tragically while on tour to sell war bonds in 1942, Lombard died in a plane crash. Although Gable remarried twice, Williams says he "was never the same." Indeed, his fifth wife buried him in Forest Lawn next to Lombard. ∎

CAROLE LOMBARD & CLARK GABLE

EVERETT COLLECTION

LAUREN *Bacall* & HUMPHREY *Bogart*

Hard-Boiled Characters, They Were Soft on Each Other

ON SCREEN, THEY PLAYED IT TOUGH AS NAILS; off-camera, though, they were tender as the night. When Betty Persky, a Jewish girl from New York City, became model Lauren Bacall and went to Hollywood in 1943, at 19, she had visions of starring opposite Cary Grant. What she got instead was a kiss—in *To Have and Have Not*—from a hard-drinking 44-year-old screen warhorse with a lived-in face and a troubled third marriage named Humphrey Bogart. Wed in 1945, they made three more films—and sparks—together. Bacall quit acting in 1950 to raise their children Stephen and Leslie, and the Bogart Holmby Hills estate became a domestic heaven. After Bogie died of cancer in 1957, Bacall would write of their years together, "Whenever I think of the word 'happy,' I think of then." ∎

"Everyone could see their love," says Steve Bogart of his parents (here in 1947).

The GI's Fave Was Unlucky in Love

IN 1941, RITA HAYWORTH POSED FOR THE MAGA-zine photo that made her the WWII pinup queen, and starred in *You'll Never Get Rich* with Fred Astaire (who, surprisingly, proclaimed her his favorite dance partner). Sadly, America's great Love Goddess, as she was known, never found her own true love. Said to have been sexually abused by her father, Hayworth careened through five marriages, notably to Orson Welles and playboy-prince Aly Khan. After 61 films, she died at 68 of Alzheimer's. A friend mused, "Actually, she was just a dancing gypsy who would have been very happy working in a chorus, happily married to some average-type husband." ■

ROCK *Hudson*

Hudson pumped up his manly image with an arranged three-year marriage.

The problem, she said (striking a comely mid-'40s pose), was that men "fell in love with [my image] and woke up with me."

RITA *Hayworth*

A Leading Man Led a Double Life

"I HOPE I DIE OF A HEART ATTACK BEFORE THEY find out," Rock Hudson said upon learning he had AIDS. However, 10 weeks before his death in 1985, the 59-year-old actor—one of the last studio-grown heartthrobs—told the world that he was gay and terminally ill. The revelation sparked an outpouring of support and research dollars. It also helped boyfriend Marc Christian (who never knew of his companion's condition) win a $5.5 million negligence suit. Hudson became the first big-name AIDS casualty. In the endgame of his life he finally stepped out of character and played himself. ■

She Needed No Translation

WITH HER SENSUAL LIPS, EROTIC POSES AND exquisite (naked!) limbs, Brigitte Bardot was too exotic a package to ignore when she burst upon the French scene in the 1956 film *And God Created Woman.* "She is not just sexy," one French magazine gasped. "She is *Le Sexe.*" For decades, Bardot played the sex kitten to purrfection, not just in scores of films but in real life too. Her four marriages were stormy, her much-publicized affairs melodramatic. At 62, she has a different focus for her fiery passion: animal rights. ∎

BRIGITTE *Bardot*

INGRID *Bergman*

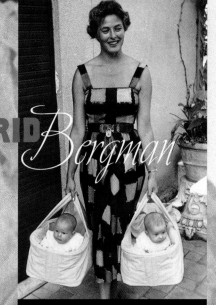

Artist Jean Cocteau called Bardot "a pouting young sphinx, but with perfect curves."

Though her flawless beauty made for what Hollywood cameramen call "bulletproof angles," Ingrid Bergman wasn't bulletproof when her extramarital affair with Italian director Roberto Rossellini erupted in scandal in 1949. Vilified on the Senate floor as "a powerful influence for evil," she was blacklisted for seven years. Before resuming her brilliant career, Bergman, who died of cancer in 1982, divorced her first husband, married Rossellini, had a son and twin girls (above, in 1952), then divorced again.

Her Stick Figure Made Olive Oyl Seem Zaftig

TOP: JOHN S. CLARKE/GLOBE PHOTOS; BOTTOM: UPI/CORBIS-BETTMANN

IN THE LATE '60s, HERS WAS THE winning combination: 31-23-31. No bust, no hips, no curves. Just 92 pounds of knock-kneed Cockney waifishness, aired on a 5' 6" frame, topped with a blonde bob and a heavily painted, glazed stare. "It's not really what you'd call a figure, is it?" Twiggy giggled at 17. Though she quit modeling after four years to move into movies, marriage and motherhood, the hold of Twiggy's androgynous appeal remained, setting a beauty standard that would frustrate fleshier females and cause eating disorders for generations to come. ■

Now 47, she says that in her superstar days, "I hated the way I looked."

TWIGGY

MASTERS & JOHNSON
They Turned Sex into a Science

TO ASSIST IN HIS 1950s LABORATORY STUDY OF human sexual response, William Masters wanted someone who was personable and smart, preferably a mother. Virginia Johnson, a thrice-divorced mom of two, wanted a campus job. Together (here, in 1966), they put sexual arousal through the scientific hoops, then pioneered treatment for couples with sex problems. Their own 21-year marriage foundered on a less-arousing dysfunction: workaholism. ■

RAQUEL

"I consider all of the roles that I have done as camp," she said after the 1970 bomb *Myra Breckinridge* (right) cast her as a transsexual.

CHRISTINE JORGENSEN

Americans were shocked, fascinated and bewildered when an ex-GI from The Bronx named George Jorgensen returned home from Denmark in 1955 with a female name—and sexual apparatus to match. The first American to publicize a sex change, Christine (here, in Rome in 1954) said before her 1989 death that she'd given the sexual revolution "a good swift kick in the pants."

WELCH

Carve Her Curves on Rushmore

IT'S NOT AS IF THE SEX GODDESS THING HAPPENED for her overnight. First she was a beauty contestant, a TV weather girl, a movie extra. But after male fingers twitched to rip deadly antibodies from her skin-diving suit in the 1966 flick *Fantastic Voyage*, Raquel Welch was launched as the Vietnam era's pinup princess. Despite three failed marriages and many more failed films, Welch's humor and curves remain intact. "My body is just there," she once said, "like Mount Rushmore." ■

WOODY ALLEN

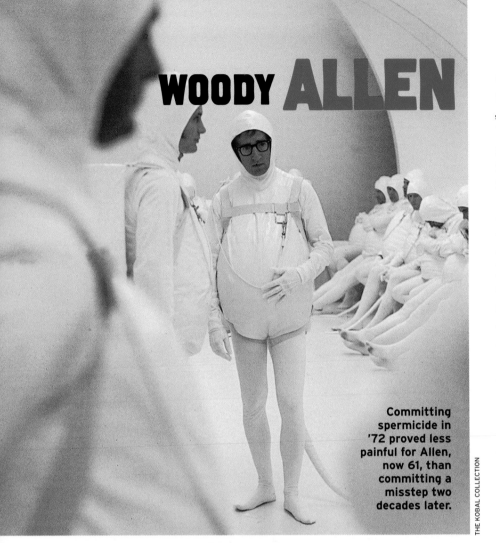

Committing spermicide in '72 proved less painful for Allen, now 61, than committing a misstep two decades later.

THE KOBAL COLLECTION

A Satirist Is Hoist On His Own Petard

WOODY ALLEN'S COMIC scripts, antic direction and star turn as a nervous sperm in 1972's *Everything You Always Wanted to Know About Sex* (*but were afraid to ask)* made us laugh at our sexual hang-ups. We allowed for his artist's license and welcomed his lady du jour in his films (including second wife Louise Lasser in *Everything)*. But after his affair with a 36-years-younger daughter of his longtime lover Mia Farrow became public in 1992, many people stopped laughing and started revisiting Allen's work with a newly jaundiced eye. Was his squabbling with Farrow in *Husbands and Wives* for real? Did his romance with a teenager in *Manhattan* presage the scandal to come? ■

Beatty enjoyed liaisons with Natalie Wood (top middle, in 1961), Michelle Phillips (top right, in 1975) and Diane Keaton (bottom middle, in 1979) before nesting with wife Annette Bening (bottom right, in 1995.) One of the few who nixed going beyond a nibble was *Shampoo* costar Carrie Fisher (aloft in 1975).

GLOBE PHOTOS(2); BOTTOM RIGHT: ARCHIVE PHOTOS/DARLENE HAMMOND

WARREN

Wickedly Wise? Yes. Every Grandma? Not

SHE'S BEEN CALLED THE BARD of Sexual Literacy, the Munchkin of the Bedroom, even Grandma Freud. But to most audiences, this 4' 7" radio shock-jockette-cum-author-cum-TV sexpert is known simply as Dr. Ruth. Since 1980, she's been raising the nation's sex IQ with a mix of candor ("Only the tiniest percentage of men have tiny penises"), comedy ("Nothing wrong with new uses for peanut butter or onion rings") and common sense ("If the talking doesn't work, the sex life is not going to work, either"). A German refugee who lost her Orthodox Jewish parents in the Holocaust, Ruth Westheimer divorced twice before settling into a happy, 35-year marriage. Still funky and spunky at 74, she has two kids and two grandchildren. ∎

RUPAUL

DR. RUTH

In 1994, Dr. Ruth reached out for RuPaul, who says, "I'm the first drag queen you can take home to meet your mom and pop."

After Three Decades, He Cut from the Chase

HE IS AMONG THE MOST RESPECTED AND VERSATILE MEN IN FILM-dom. Actor. Screenwriter. Director. Producer. But Warren Beatty is destined to be best remembered in Hollywood as the Casanova of the Century. "The boy was out to kiss 'em all," actress Diane Ladd once said. As insatiable as he was insouciant, Beatty slayed the ladies both onscreen and off, and often managed both at the same time. He's been linked with Susan Strasberg, Jean Seberg, Leslie Caron, Joan Collins, Julie Christie, Barbra Streisand, Britt Ekland, Joni Mitchell, Carly Simon, Mary Tyler Moore, Isabelle Adjani, Madonna—not to mention the gallery at left. Beatty's three-decade rampage as a lothario ended in 1992 when he married his *Bugsy* costar, Annette Bening. They now have three kids, and Daddy has turned 60. ∎

BEATTY

The Real *Playboy* Philosophy: Work!

IN THE HEYDAY OF *PLAYBOY*, faithful oglers would have been shocked to learn that founder Hugh Hefner had neither the time nor the inclination to pursue the lascivious lifestyle celebrated in his taboo-smashing glossy. This son of rigid Methodist parents was actually a loner who often fell asleep at his own fabled parties, a can of diet cola in hand. (At right, he struts for the 1966 opening of the London Playboy Club.) No hidebound chauvinist, Hefner turned his empire over to daughter Christie in 1988. Then at 63 he wed the 1989 Playmate of the Year. Another fantasy trip? No, said the father of two tykes, "Seeing toys in the mansion, I get teary-eyed." ■

HUGH *Hefner*

ARCHIVE PHOTOS

TOM *Cruise*

Cruise oozes universal appeal. "Guys want to be like him," notes one producer, "and girls want to be with him."

He Flies High As Box-Office Top Gun

HE GOT HIS BREAKTHROUGH shot in 1983's *Risky Business* because director Paul Brickman liked his "combination of heat and innocence." With last year's *Jerry Maguire*, Tom Cruise displayed his deepening dimension and snagged an Oscar nomination. A boyish 34, he was one of four children in a struggling broken family with no child support. Money was so tight they once wrote one another poems as Christmas gifts. Life should be cushier for his own two kids in a seemingly solid second marriage to Nicole Kidman. Hollywood's most bankable hunk, Cruise is now in the $20-million-per-picture bracket. ■

DUCLOS/BENAINOUS/GAMMA LIAISON

Jagger luxuriated in his own sensuality while filming *Performance* in 1970, two years before TIME dubbed him the gender-bending "king bitch of rock."

MICK *Jagger*

Mr. Raunch 'n' Roll Got His Ya-Ya's Out

As RINGMASTER OF THE ROLLing Stones, Mick Jagger worked the primal-energy alleys of the '60s, dabbling in androgyny, showing sympathy for the devil. A promoter who once booked the Stones admitted he "didn't know whether to laugh at them or send for an animal trainer." Jagger became the marathon man of rock. But his wild-child act is wearing thin: Wife Jerry Hall reportedly ordered Mick to mend his stray-cat ways, proving even middle-age sex machines can't always get what they want. ∎

LEFT: CECIL BEATON/GLOBE PHOTOS; RIGHT: I.C. RAPOPORT

HELEN GURLEY BROWN

After her 1962 *Sex and the Single Girl* proved a bestseller, Helen Gurley Brown found her calling: "To help single women be reassured that they're okay." In her climb from mouseburger secretary to legendary editor of *Cosmopolitan*, Brown embodied the ethic of the Cosmo Girl who, she insisted, must aim to "get everything out of life—the money, recognition, success, men, prestige, authority, dignity." And, of course, great sex.

Blue Eyes Can Be Lethal Weapons

THERE'S A CLAUSE IN MEL GIBSON'S CONtracts that says he gets paid extra (a rumored $5 million for *Lethal Weapon 3*) whenever he sheds his threads onscreen. Even so, acting pal Sam Neill insists, "Mel is a character actor trapped inside a leading man's body." There are worse places to be imprisoned. The American-born, Aussie-bred father of six could coast on his rugged looks, but by taking risks in *Hamlet* and his 1995 Oscar winner *Braveheart* he has proved his heavy mettle. Off the set, Gibson's boozing and brawling years are behind him, thanks to Alcoholics Anonymous—and wife Robyn. "My Rock of Gibraltar," says the 41-year-old actor-director. "Only more beautiful." ∎

"Just a bloke," one *Braveheart* extra called the folksy star.

MEL *Gibson*

Creator of the Hit 'Dumb Blonde,' She Isn't One

WITH HER HOURGLASS FIGURE, TEASED tresses and blinding sequins, Dolly Parton presents herself as the ditzy cousin of Daisy Mae. One of 12 children of a Tennessee dirt farmer, she is, however, nobody's fool. With her formidable talents for singing, songwriting ("I Will Always Love You"), comic acting (*9 to 5*) and business, Parton moves agilely between stage, screen and boardroom. Her ventures include a music publishing company, the 93-acre Dollywood amusement park in the Great Smoky Mountains, a partnership in a production company and a 31-year marriage. At 51, this "Dumb Blonde" (the title of her '67 hit single) is one of the wealthiest women in show business. ∎

Parton (in 1996) says, "I sort of patterned my look from storybooks and the trash in our hometown."

DOLLY *Parton*

TINA *Turner*

TT Keeps On Churning

HER SWEAT-STAINED, R&B sound was forged in the *Ike and Tina Turner Revue*, which spent years ripping up pocket-size black clubs before achieving crossover fame in the mid-'60s. But as her husband Ike became increasingly abusive, "I was living a life of death," Tina recalled. In 1976 she walked away. Her personal and professional rebirth was later turned into the hit film *What's Love Got to Do With It?* And at 57, the woman Mick Jagger credits with teaching him how to dance is as sultry as ever, still bumping and grinding to the beat of "Proud Mary." As one critic notes, a song about a stately riverboat is "an exhilarating metaphor for Miss Turner's staying power." ∎

The winner of seven Grammies cashed in on what she calls her "strange little gutsy kind of voice."

NICOLA DILL/OUTLINE

"Most of all, I had the impression of someone who was a cripple inside."
—*East of Eden* director Elia Kazan

GONE TOO SOON

They flamed brightly and briefly across the century's firmament, leaving legacies that fascinate us still

FEBRUARY 8,1931–SEPTEMBER 30,1955

JAMES DEAN

Starring in just three films, he became–and remains–our icon of the tortured soul of youth

EVERY FEW YEARS, "A NEW JAMES DEAN" IS PROCLAIMED– think Leonardo DiCaprio, Luke Perry–but none has ever touched the charisma of the original. In *Rebel Without a Cause,* *Giant* and *East of Eden,* the Indiana farm boy's mannerisms–the troubled sneer, the inarticulate yearnings, the explosive sexuality lurking beneath an affecting innocence–connected with 1950s adolescents like nothing before or since. In party-mad Hollywood, Dean was a disheveled and strung-out insomniac who explored all corners of the sexual garden and imbibed like Jett Rink, his *Giant* character. He once showed up drunk at the door of actress Ann Doran, who played his *Rebel* mother, shouting, "Mom! Mom! It's your son!" Dean's death at 24 was as enigmatic and symbolic as his life: He crashed his speeding Porsche 550 Spyder on a rural California road. ■

Dean (in 1954) "seemed shrouded in a moodiness and a misery," wrote a biographer.

JUDY GARLAND

The magic of her personality inspired a cult of pathos

SHE NEVER MADE IT OVER THE rainbow. Blessed with a voluminous, music-hall voice, talent to spare and a disarming sincerity, the young *Wizard of Oz* star nevertheless turned increasingly to drugs and alcohol to assuage the insecurities magnified by her driven stage mother, even in Judy's adulthood, and the furious pace of studio work. She married five fractious times and did her best to mother children Liza Minnelli and Lorna and Joseph Luft. Amid some 35 movies, albums and wrenching concerts, she suffered suicide attempts, breakdowns and illnesses. Her performances, said one critic, became "tribal celebrations," which had fans chanting, "We love you, Judy!" But the adulation was not enough. Before she died of an overdose of barbiturates at 47, she said of the making of *Oz*, "I was really little tortured Tillie in the whole damn thing." ∎

> "I have a truly great love of an audience, and I used to want to prove it to them by giving them blood."

"We made up as hard as we fought," recalled husband Charlie Dick of Cline (in an undated photo). "We had a lot of fun making up."

Garland (opposite page, performing on a TV show in 1961) told friends after her 1965 divorce from producer Sid Luft that she felt "like I am living in a blizzard."

SEPTEMBER 8, 1932–MARCH 5, 1963

PATSY CLINE

She gave her fans 'Sweet Dreams,' but didn't get to live them

PATSY CLINE ONLY RECORDED FOR EIGHT YEARS AND NEVER MADE enough money to hire her own band. But three decades after a plane crash ended her life, the singer is a country-and-western cash machine. Her posthumous greatest hits album has been on *Billboard*'s country chart more than 10 years; and with it, she became the first female artist to sell 6 million copies of one album. With hits like "Crazy" and "I Fall to Pieces," she became the first female country vocalist to scale both pop and country charts. Her blend of rockabilly, gospel, pop and blues presaged the crossover country sound, influencing Loretta Lynn and Cline-clone LeAnn Rimes. A native Virginian, Cline was sexually abused by her father, left school at 16, and had two unhappy marriages. The hard times made her leather-tough. As country singer Tommy O'Day said, "Patsy could tell you to go to hell just as fast as George Jones." ∎

JEAN **HARLOW**

Scandal scarred the original 'Blonde Bombshell'

"I have lost a friend," said Louis B. Mayer after her death. "The world has lost a ray of sunlight."

"All I've got is a lot of talent and plenty of chutzpah."

"HOW DO YOU LIKE TO WAKE up in the morning?" a reporter once asked her. "I like to wake up feeling a new man," she quipped. No wonder she was dubbed the Blonde Bombshell. Under a helmet of platinum hair, Jean Harlow slithered across the screen with a libidinous smile and a quick retort in sizzling classics like *Red Dust* and *Hell's Angels.* Blatantly sensual—she sometimes drove to the studio wearing a mink coat over pajamas—she shocked and fascinated Depression-era America. Raised in the Midwest by her mother and stepfather (father Mont Clair Carpenter, a dentist, left the family), Harlow was at 21 anointed by a columnist "Hollywood's reigning sex goddess." Her crown, however, was irreversibly tarnished in 1932. Second husband Paul Bern, 42, an MGM executive, took off his clothes and shot himself. A suicide note suggested he was impotent. Harlow wed again a year later, but the marriage lasted only eight months. At 26, after battling kidney disease treated only by the Christian Science prayers of her mother, the goddess died of uremic poisoning. ■

Harlow (left, in the '30s) was called by Fred Astaire "a fine artist and one of Hollywood's most beloved citizens."

Some writers held that Gershwin's songs were fully realized only when he did the playing (here in 1930).

SEPTEMBER 26, 1898 – JULY 11, 1937

GEORGE
GERSHWIN

A sad master of song, he strove to capture the American spirit and elevate it to popular art

GEORGE GERSHWIN WAS A PRODIGY IN A HURRY—WHICH, sadly, proved providential since his life was cut short at 38 by a brain tumor diagnosed too late to save him. A rowdy and truant youth, Gershwin quit high school in New York City to pursue music. By rapid turns a theater-rehearsal pianist, vaudeville accompanist and publishing-house staff composer, he was just 20 when he wrote his first Broadway musical. Often in collaboration with his older brother, lyricist Ira, Gershwin scored more than two dozen films and shows. Though he was hailed for his orchestral *Rhapsody In Blue* in 1924, Gershwin later was spurned by the classical music critics whose approval he craved. But, then, he was used to rejection: His own parents disparaged his accomplishments throughout his life. ■

JIMI HENDRIX

He kissed the sky with sounds never heard before, but his castles were made of sand

THE MOST ASTONISHING GUI-tarist of the '60s—raised in Seattle by a Cherokee mother and a black father—left a legacy as mixed as the decade his music reflected. Musicians speak with awe of the still-inimitable effects Jimi Hendrix wrought with bare-bones equipment. ("How he did this," guitar ace Mike Bloomfield later said, "I wish I understood.") Hendrix's electrifying showmanship—he played his guitar with his teeth or behind his back, then set it on fire—ignited fans. But there was also the womanizing musician, arrested in 1969 on unproven charges of heroin possession, who a year later choked to death on his own vomit, caused by a barbiturate overdose. Hendrix gave the world "Purple Haze"—then, at 27, he died in one. ∎

Hendrix (in 1968) was shy offstage. "Everyone took, took, took from Jimi," said band-mate Noel Redding. "The only things they gave were drugs."

"When I die I'm not going to have a funeral. I'm going to have a jam session. And, knowing me, I'll probably get busted at my own funeral."

JANIS JOPLIN

Heroin took more than a piece of her heart

SHRIEKING OUT HER EARTHY SONGS, SWIGGING Southern Comfort onstage, shooting up to stave off boredom, Janis Joplin lived hard. The Port Arthur, Texas, native made her name with Big Brother and the Holding Company and then went solo. But disappointed by a philandering fiancé and increasingly lonely, Joplin sank deeper into drug abuse. At 27, she was found dead of a heroin overdose, the needle marks still fresh on her arm. Ironically, Joplin never had a No. 1 record until her rendition of Kris Kristofferson's *Me and Bobby McGee* was released posthumously in 1971. ■

> "Maybe I won't last as long as other singers, but you can destroy your *now* worrying about tomorrow."

Joplin lolled in 1969 at New York City's famously arty and seedy Chelsea Hotel.

DAVID GAHR

THOMAS D. MCAVOY/LIFE

MAY 7, 1919 – JULY 26, 1952

EVA PERÓN

A ruthless actress turned first lady created a cult–and got rich–championing the poor

SHE WAS THE BASTARD CHILD OF A RANCHER AND his cook. But Eva Duarte, a vivacious actress, gained instant legitimacy by marrying then-Colonel Juan Perón and helping propel him to Argentina's presidency in 1946. He hogged the power. She got the glory, fighting for women and redistributing wealth to the poor. Together they also stocked a Swiss bank account. Their demagogic tango ended when Evita died of cancer. Supporters begged the Vatican to make her a saint. Opponents stole her body to frustrate cultists. Almost 25 years passed before she was laid to rest by Juan, safely buried under three layers of steel plate. ∎

"People see Eva Perón as either a saint or the incarnation of Satan. I can definitely identify with her."
—Madonna, who played her in the '96 film

"I can walk around it, work from the four sides, and really be *in* the painting."

JANUARY 28, 1912 – AUGUST 11, 1956

JACKSON POLLOCK

A troubled painter wrestled his demons to the canvas

JACKSON POLLOCK DISPENSED WITH THE TOOLS AS WELL AS THE RULES of art. He chucked easel and palette, preferring to spread the canvas across the studio floor and attack it, often with sticks or basters instead of brushes. Departing from his realist mentor, Thomas Hart Benton, the Wyoming native developed "action painting," heralding Abstract Expressionism and helping establish New York City as the capital of avant-garde art in the 1940s. "In him," declared authoritative critic Clement Greenberg, "we had truth." But like his work, Pollock was a swirl of emotion. He had one breakdown, struggled with alcoholism and died at 44 in a head-on crash of his convertible that mirrored the violence captured in his rawest paintings. ∎

HANS NAMUTH

FEBRUARY 6,1945—MAY 11,1981

BOB MARLEY

*With Rastaman vibration, he inspired
Jamaica, then the world, to catch a fire*

IT SEEMED A CRUDE IRONY. AS THE TARGET
of Jamaica's political gangs, he'd survived a spray of
bullets in 1976, only to be struck down five years
later, at 36, by brain cancer. Though Bob Marley
dominated Jamaica's reggae scene only a short
time, his legacy remains unchallenged. At home,
where Marley steered clear of party politics, his
songs spoke to and for the poorest in his island
nation. Abroad, Marley, a devout Rastafarian,
made reggae converts of Americans and Euro-
peans with his uniquely danceable blend of R&B,
soul, rock and folk. Today, Marley's son
Ziggy, 28, carries on
the tradition. ∎

APRIL 7, 1915 – JULY 17, 1959

BILLIE HOLIDAY

Lady lived the blues, and with teasing charm and sublime pathos lifted jazz singing to new plateaus

HER LANGUID TONES RESONATE TODAY IN THE VOICES OF Cassandra Wilson, Abbey Lincoln and Carmen Lundy. Frank Sinatra once admitted he learned phrasing from her. "Billie Holiday's voice was the voice of living intensity," wrote critic Leonard Feather. Her sound reflected the sadness of her life. Born in Baltimore to teenage parents (her father was an itinerant guitarist), Holiday was raped at 10 and scrubbed floors in a brothel before trying to become a dancer. Her life turned around when a sympathetic audition pianist asked if she could sing. Holiday landed her first Harlem nightclub job in 1931. She toured briefly with Count Basie and Artie Shaw, but was worn down by the racism she encountered in hotels and clubs. Her first husband, ne'er-do-well James Monroe, abused her, squandered her money and introduced her to heroin, which became the curse of her life. Holiday was jailed on drug charges in 1947 and as a result lost her New York City cabaret license despite a triumphant return to the stage at Carnegie Hall. She died at 44 of heart and kidney failure with only 70 cents in the bank. ∎

Marley (in 1980) won the United Nations Peace Medal in 1978 for his humanitarian efforts.

Sinatra called Holiday (in '47) "the most important influence on American popular singing."

BUDDY HOLLY

Though he was memorialized in 'the day the music died,' his rockabilly classics live on

IN HIS TORQUEY FALSETTO, BUDDY HOLLY chirped out many of the groundbreaking hits of rockabilly, including "That'll Be the Day," "Peggy Sue" and "Maybe Baby." Constantly on the road (sometimes with his group, the Crickets), he ranked almost with Elvis until his plane went down in an Iowa snowstorm in 1959. Perishing with him were Ritchie Valens and the Big Bopper. In "American Pie," Don McLean paid tribute to February 3 as "the day the music died." Holly was 22, and he left his bride of six months, Marie Elena Santiago. Earlier, the Texas-born Holly toured Britain, and his pluck-and-strum guitar style influenced the rock invaders of the '60s. Fittingly, Paul McCartney bought the publishing rights to Buddy's tunes. ∎

> "I don't have the time."
> —The refrain his widow recalls him using too often

JIM HENSON

With his soft voice and inspired menagerie, a gentle genius became the Pied Piper of children's TV

> "He was our era's Chaplin, W.C. Fields and Marx Brothers."
> —Joan Ganz Cooney, past president, Children's Television Workshop

TO KIDS EVERYWHERE, JIM HENSON'S MISS Piggy, Kermit the Frog and Fozzie Bear may be more intriguing and beloved than any human celebrities. Which made it all the more wrenching in 1990 when, at 53, he died suddenly after a severe bout of pneumonia. The Mississippi-born father of five created in *Sesame Street* perhaps the most influential children's program ever. Seven years later, in 1976, *The Muppet Show* was born, followed by a string of movies. At his funeral, while 5,000 fans fluttered hand-painted butterflies, a Dixieland band stomped out a rousing *When the Saints Go Marching In.* ∎

Her Serene Highness considered acting again, but said, "I don't have the time to devote to it."

"She took her experience as an actress and applied it to being a princess, a wife and a mother."—Bridesmaid Judy Quine

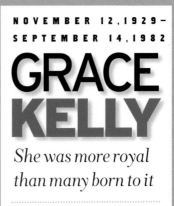

NOVEMBER 12, 1929 – SEPTEMBER 14, 1982

GRACE KELLY

She was more royal than many born to it

"I CERTAINLY DON'T think of my life as a fairy tale," she once said, but Grace Kelly did live an enchanted existence. The Philadelphia debutante moved in a monied realm of screen stars and royalty and proved that a girl could succeed in both worlds. As an actress she projected what director Alfred Hitchcock called "sexual elegance" in such cinematic gems as *Rear Window*, *To Catch a Thief* and *The Country Girl*, for which she won an Academy Award in 1955. When she retired to wed Prince Rainier of Monaco in 1956, Grace worked tirelessly promoting her adopted country and turned down film offers to focus on raising her three children, Prince Albert and Princesses Caroline and Stephanie. Her 1982 death, at 52, in a car accident driving home with Stephanie, left the world bereft. ■

RYAN WHITE

His light shone in the darkness of AIDS

HE NEVER SURRENDERED—NOT TO AIDS, not to despair, not to the fearful public passions that his illness once aroused. Diagnosed in 1984 with AIDS contracted through a tainted tranfusion for his hemophilia, Ryan White successfully challenged his school board in Kokomo, Indiana, for the right to attend classes and found himself a reluctant celebrity. Making friends of stars such as Elton John and Michael Jackson, the stalwart teen traveled throughout the U.S. and Europe promoting AIDS awareness. He had moved with his sister Andrea and factory-worker mother Jeanne to nearby Cicero, Indiana, in hope of finding a more ordinary childhood. But Ryan White was not ordinary. With his smile and grace, he taught the world not to give in to fear. ■

> "It was Ryan who first humanized the disease called AIDS."—His minister, Raymond Probasco

The funeral of White (seen here five years before his death at 18) was attended by First Lady Barbara Bush.

JULY 10,1943–FEBRUARY 6,1993

ARTHUR ASHE

Pioneer and paragon, the tennis great lacked only a stroke of luck

HE ROSE FROM THE SEGREGATED COURTS OF RICHMOND, VIRGINIA, TO the hallowed ground of Wimbledon. Arthur Ashe was the first black to become a mainstay (and a champion) on the men's pro circuit, and epitomized a near-extinct species: the articulate, socially aware athlete. Heart disease cut short his career at 37. Ashe contracted AIDS from tainted blood following bypass surgery in 1983, but didn't show symptoms until five years later. "Despair is a state of mind," he declared, "to which I refuse to give in." He remained active in political causes, started an AIDS foundation and wrote a memoir, *Days of Grace*. He and wife Jeanne, a photographer, also prepared their 7-year-old daughter, Camera, for the inevitable, and Arthur wrote her letters to remember him by. ■

Ashe (in 1991) was a student-athlete before and after his days at UCLA. His mother, Mattie, died when Arthur was still in grade school, and he later noted, "Books and sports were my way of bandaging the wound."

"The best way to judge a life is to ask yourself, 'Did I make the best use of the time I had?' "

Bruce (in '63) was
played by Dustin
Hoffman in the
'74 bioflick *Lenny*.
Howard Stern saw
it on his first date
with wife Alison.

> "Lenny lived so that old ladies today can talk like he talked."
> —His comedienne mother, Sally Marr

OCTOBER 13, 1925–AUGUST 3, 1966

LENNY BRUCE

He believed his so-called sick comedy could be a
social healer, but along the way it helped kill him

HE JOLTED THE CLUB CIRCUIT IN THE '50s AND '60s WITH
a brand of subversive, corrosive satire that cleared the way for outrage artists from Woody Allen to Joan Rivers. His jazzy, expletive-
laced riffs slashed to the heart of politics, religion, racism and sex.
His personal life also defied convention. The son of a pioneering
stand-up, Sally Marr, he was raised on Long Island, New York,
left school in eighth grade, joined the Navy, briefly studied acting,
married a stripper and developed an unkickable drug habit.

Obscenity law was tighter in his day, and he was frequently
busted, twice deported from Britain and, in 1964, ruled "patently
offensive" by a New York court. Hundreds of supporters from
John Updike to theologian Reinhold Niebuhr signed a protest
declaring him "in the tradition of Swift, Rabelais and Twain."
But by then Bruce was broke and unraveling. When he died, at
40, a needle in his arm in his Hollywood home, the official cause
of death was morphine poisoning. Admirers believed he OD'd
on harassment. ■

JOHN BELUSHI

Too much wasn't enough for the kamikaze comic

BACK IN WHEATON, ILLINOIS, JOHN BELUSHI WON A citizenship medal in eighth grade, which was about the last time he behaved himself. He once advised younger brother Jim, then a struggling actor, "Go out onstage like a bull in a ring." Indeed, that's exactly how Belushi charged into the spotlight in 1975 as part of the original cast of *Saturday Night Live.* Belushi's gonzo physicality produced the samurai dry cleaner; the "Cheeseburger, Cheeseburger" hash slinger; the bandito Killer Bee. He was Jackie Gleason with a raging id. *National Lampoon's Animal House,* the first of his seven films, grossed out America while grossing $200 million. Though happily married to high school sweetheart Judith Jacklin, Belushi remained "a party monster," admitted pal Dan Aykroyd. The party ended in a funky Hollywood hotel bungalow, where police found the comic's naked body. Cathy Smith, the dealer-to-the-stars who injected him with the fatal heroin-cocaine "speedball," sold her story to a tabloid for $15,000, then did 15 months in jail. ■

On the *SNL* set (in '75) Belushi delighted in ad hoc daffyness. "We used to be immobile with laughter," recalled Dan Aykroyd.

"Now rock 'n' roll is at a standstill, I think—and comedy is taking its place as something exciting."

MADDY MILLER

JUNE 28,1946—MAY 20,1989

GILDA RADNER

It was always something, and we treasured every minute of it

AS ONE OF *SATURDAY NIGHT LIVE'S* ORIGINAL NOT READY FOR PRIME-time Players, Gilda Radner propagated her own species of characters: flat-chested nerd Lisa Loopner, frizzy-haired gross-out expert Roseanne Roseannadanna and lisping super-interviewer Baba Wawa. "Like Dickens, she's added people to the world who bear her stamp," wrote a *New York Times* critic. A Detroit native, Radner got her sense of humor from her father, Herman, a hotel proprietor who died when she was 14. Radner went from TV to Broadway to Hollywood, where she met and married comic actor Gene Wilder. Their hopes of starting a family were dashed when Radner was diagnosed with ovarian cancer in 1986. For 2½ years she valiantly battled what she called "the most unfunny thing in the world." After she died at 42, Wilder established the Gilda's Club cancer support network in her memory. ∎

"I wanted to crawl into the coffin . . . and have them close the lid and bury me with her."
—Her husband, Chris Pérez

APRIL 16, 1971 –
MARCH 31, 1995

SELENA

She became the queen of Tex-Mex song but never strayed from her fans

SHE WAS KNOWN AS THE Madonna of Tejano music, and onstage Selena was flirtatious and passionate. But it was the fact that she was so proudly *del pueblo*–"of the people"– that forged the powerful, personal bond with her audience. Singing on the road with her brother and sister from the age of 10, she had become, by 23, wealthy, famous and on the cusp of crossover stardom. Yet she and her husband, guitarist Chris Pérez, still lived next door to her folks in the modest Molina neighborhood of Corpus Christi, Texas.

That year, 1995, her vibrant life was cut tragically short when she was shot by Yolanda Saldívar, the ex-president of her fan club whom she had just confronted for embezzling funds. Selena's posthumous album *Dreaming of You* went multiplatinum and completed her breakthrough into the Anglo market. ∎

"She had so much magnetism and charisma," recalled Jeremy Leven, who directed Selena (in 1994) in *Don Juan DeMarco*, her first and only film.

151

GLENN GOULD

His dazzling idiosyncratic stamp created genuine Shine

> "If there's any excuse at all for making a record, it's to do it differently, to perform this work as it has never been heard before."

BLACK STAR

THE LIST OF HIS ECCENTRICI-
ties ran as long as his talent.
Glenn Gould wore overcoats in
the summer, soaked his hands in
hot water before performing and
preferred to sit low at the piano,
almost shoulder-level with the
keyboard. When the gifted vir-
tuoso declared, "The concert is
dead" and gave up public performance in 1964, many thought it
was another incarnation of his
whimsy. But Gould embarked on
an extraordinary studio career
and for the next 18 years until his
untimely death of a stroke at age
50, the Toronto-born son of a
furrier would make nearly 80
recordings considered, according to the *New York Times*,
"among the most significant and
challenging musical documents
of our time." From Bach's *Goldberg Variations*, in 1956, to
Brahms, Hayden and Schoen-
berg, Gould explored a vast
repertoire using a film director's
approach of taping parts of
music out of sequence and splic-
ing them together at the editor's
table. Critics sometimes found
the results cold but, wrote biographer Otto Friedrich, Gould's
intellectually rigorous performances had "a power that made
many people feel that their lives
had somehow been changed,
deepened, enriched." ∎

**Gould (in 1967)
once said,
"At live con-
certs I feel
demeaned, like
a vaudevillian."**

Plath (in 1955)
was able, wrote
critic Janet
Malcolm, "to
confront what
most of us
fearfully shrank
from."

UPI/CORBIS-BETTMANN

OCTOBER 27,1932–FEBRUARY 11,1963

SYLVIA PLATH

*In wrenching, sexually tormented poems, she
prefigured her own breakdown and suicide*

"DADDY, DADDY, YOU BASTARD, I'M
through." With a single line of verse, a precocious, deeply troubled Bostonian electrified
American poetry in 1965 and became a femi-
nist touchstone. The daughter of a Boston University professor, Sylvia Plath was once con-
fined to a mental hospital. She soared in her
autobiographical writing that explored emo-
tional and verbal abuse. Her celebrated novel
The Bell Jar detailed a neurotic young woman's
descent into illness and near-suicide. At 30, she
succeeded in her own second attempt, by
gassing herself in her London oven, while her
two young children by estranged husband Ted
Hughes, England's poet laureate, slept nearby. ∎

**"Beware
Beware.
Out of the ash
I rise with my
red hair
And I eat men
like air."
—From *Lady
Lazarus***

THE TITANIC

It perished 85 years ago, and the world is still rubbernecking

WHY IS IT THAT DECADES AFTER SINKING INTO SALTY OBLIVION, THE *TITANIC* continues to resurface in books and movies—and people's nightmares? Is it the sheer magnitude of the toll—1,513 lives lost in one place at one time? Or is it the jarring confrontation of expectations versus experience? The ship was the largest, most luxurious liner ever built and heralded as unsinkable. But less than three hours after hitting an iceberg south of Newfoundland, it went down amid panic and horrible screams that forever haunted the survivors. To be sure, scientists have kept the tragedy fresh: A 1985 expedition yielded the first shots of the wreckage 2.5 miles below the surface; a 1996 study suggested that it wasn't a 300-ft. gash but six small wounds that caused the fatal gush. Even so, it's the human detail—and hubris—that most haunts and fascinates. Why, after receiving warnings of "bergs, growlers and field ice," did the lookouts not use binoculars? Why was the 882-ft.-long vessel outfitted with only 20 lifeboats, when it was designed to carry 48? Why were all the children from first class, save one, among the 700 survivors, yet 49 children in steerage perished? Life, as John F. Kennedy said, is unfair. So is death. ∎

First-class passengers (above) boarded in Southampton, England (left), and paid today's equivalent of almost $50,000 per suite—one way. This eerie underwater shot (right) showed the *Titanic*'s bow railing in 1991.